The Super Dan Method of Free-Fighting

Taking Your Skills To The Next Level

Prof. Dan Anderson - 10th Dan

US National & World Free-Fighting Champion

Joe Lewis Eternal Warrior Award Recipient

The Super Dan Method of Free-Fighting

Taking Your Skills To The Next Level

Prof. Dan Anderson - 10th Dan

US National & World Free-Fighting Champion

Joe Lewis Eternal Warrior Recipient

Contacting Dan Anderson

Website: http://www.danandersonbooksndvds.com

Email: dannyleeanderson@hotmail.com

Postal Mail: P.O. Box 1463 • Gresham, Oregon 97030

Warning

This book is presented only as a means of presenting a unique aspect of the art of karate. The author does not make any representation, warranty or guarantee that the techniques described or illustrated in this book will be safe or effective in any self-defense situation or otherwise. You may be injured if you apply or train the techniques illustrated in this book. To minimize the risk of training injury, nothing described or illustrated in this book should be undertaken without personal, expert instruction. In addition, it is essential that you consult a physician regarding whether or not to attempt anything described in this book. Specific self-defense responses illustrated in this book may not be justified in any particular situation in view if all the circumstances or under the applicable federal, state or local law.

ACKNOWLEDGEMENTS

As I write this I have been involved in martial art for 51 years - over half a century! How can I possibly thank and acknowledge everyone who has been an influence in my career? I can't. Everyone who I have trained with, watched, fought and read about has had some impact on my martial arts in one way or another. There are several people who I will single out, though.

My thanks to Loren Christensen, Mike Engeln and Bruce Terrill, who were my principle instructors in karate.

My thanks to Remy Presas and Ted Buot, who were my principle instructors in Filipino Martial Arts, which has impacted my karate tremendously.

My thanks to my brothers in martial arts: Bram Frank, Brian Zawilinski, Fred King, Johnny Olivera and Jeff Burger.

My thanks to many of the Top Ten karate champions who patiently listened to and answered my many questions - Jeff Smith, Howard Jackson, Bill Wallace, Chuck Norris, Al Dacascos, Joe Lewis, Steve Muhammad (formerly Sanders) to name a few.

My thanks to my Top Ten peers, from whom I learned a great deal as well - Keith Vitali, Raymond McCallum, Linda Denley, Arlene Limas, Mike Genova, Bobby Tucker, Jimmy Tabares and many others.

My thanks to dear friends who have departed - Steve Armstrong, my mentor for so many years. Steve Fisher, my friend and brother. Larry Kelly, the East Coast version of my rebellious self.

My thanks to Lee Wedlake, Jeff Burger for their initial scrutiny and suggestions to this book.

My thanks to Kirby Barker for his ruthless editing of my text.

My thanks to Ashley Stading for being my photo partner. She came in many early mornings to shoot the video footage with me from which the stills for this book were taken.

My thanks to my wife, Marie, who put up with my being absorbed in this project for many, many hours.

My thanks to L. Ron Hubbard, whose discoveries in the realm of man have influenced me profoundly.

Table Of Contents

Forewords

I first saw Dan Anderson fight back when we were both on the national circuit. Here was a man who didn't wear a gi top but a shirt with a Superman emblem on the chest. Back then, that was a little unconventional since traditionalists still ruled the rings but things were changing. In this book, Dan tells of the changes in sport karate and he's correct in the telling. He was right in the middle of it.

Being that I was a rated competitor, I would often be able to get a front-row seat at the finals. I sat ringside in Chicago at the American Karate Association Grand Nationals when Keith Vitali, from Atlanta, and Super Dan punched it out for Grand Champion. They were both fast, technical and they were talking to each other as they fought. I heard "Gotcha!", "No, you didn't!" followed by furious exchanges. It was something to see.

Fast forward to the early to mid-1980s and I was in the offices of *Inside Kung-Fu* magazine in Hollywood, California, talking with the editor. They were partnered with Unique Publications and we were discussing the possibility of publishing a book I was working on. When he asked me what I had in mind I told him I planned to model it on Dan's book, *American Freestyle Karate*, which was not a typical "picture book" on doing karate. Without hesitation, he said it was the best book written on the subject, and both of us smiled and nodded in agreement. (My book was never published by Unique but years later I published a series on Ed Parker's Kenpo, keeping that same goal in mind.)

I was surprised and honored that Dan would ask me to look over this manuscript and that he asked me to write this foreword. Reading it, I found we had similar backgrounds in the art, were driven to discover and apply, became successful in competition and went on to teach and write. He's done a great job with this book and I found several nuggets of valuable information for myself. I believe the formula he passes on here will benefit not only the target audience of older students of the art but also the "young-uns" who will eventually move to the senior divisions. The proverb, "Only change is changeless", applies to us when we see we have to alter our training methods when we see we sometimes can't do what we used to do as well as we could, as Dan points out in the book. He offers solutions and has proven they work.

It's a read and re-read book, worthy of highlights and underlines. Now get out there and work.

Lee Wedlake
9th Degree Black
Ed Parker's Kenpo Karate

One of the best most comprehensive books I have ever read on not just the history of fighting, but the applications of fighting principles and strategies. This book offers so much material that carries over into all aspects of fighting. I will recommend this book to all the fighters and students I train, as there is no doubt it is based on many years of thought and actual success in real time applications by one of the All Time Greats in the Game. Truly great read!
Kirby Barker

I first heard of Professor Dan Anderson in mid-1980's via his first book "American Freestyle Karate". That book changed my fight game and mindset towards learning. Later I met and trained with Prof Dan in his MA-80 (Modern Arnis) program. He changed my stick game. He has changed my trapping game. Quick back story, I accumulated almost 2 years training in China and a man from a small town in Oregon changed my trapping game. (Let that sink in)

Professor Dan is one of those teachers who can whittle the information down to the essentials and now he has done it with his latest work "Super Dan Method of Free-Fighting".

Super Dan Method of Free-Fighting, short version, one of USA's top 10 Karate fighters uses his knowledge and experience to develop a sparring art that can work in your senior years.
He proves it by successfully competing in his mid-60's, even against the young guns.

The book also contains some great research and history on how Karate tournament sparring developed to what it is today.

He also busts one of the biggest martial arts myths - "You can't learn from books or videos"
Professor Dan talks about his own experience of living in a small town with no access to big name instructors and learning from books and magazines. Sure, having a live teacher to instruct and correct you is better, but you can learn from other sources.

Remember, he became one of USA's top 10 Karate fighters.

I have been in the martial arts for over 35 years, I have lived and trained in China, Thailand...and I still took knowledge away from this book.

Jeff Burger
5th Degree Black Belt Shito Ryu Karate
5th Degree Black Belt Matsukazi Ryu Ju Jutsu
Muay Thai Kru, trained and certified in Thailand
2006 Silver Medalist Full Contact Kick Boxing World Championships

Author's Forward

My qualifications for writing this book...

Why am I qualified to write a book on free-fighting? Is it because I am a national champion in free-fighting? Not really, but it helps. How about because I am pretty literate and can put concepts into words that people can understand? Again, no, but that helps as well. How about because I am a very analytical practitioner of the martial arts? Nope.

So, why am I qualified to write this book? There are two reasons. The first is that when I began my karate training, I was afraid of getting hit. Deathly afraid. I was not a natural fighter. That was my brother, Don. I was a natural runner. A little known fact is that I failed my first karate belt test, my blue stripe test, because of my lack of sparring ability. I passed the kata (prearranged solo exercise) portion of it but failed the sparring portion.

The second reason is that my karate career began in a local recreation center taught by two under belts. I did not grow up in a school run by established champions. I had to research and read everything I could get my hands on to learn winning moves. *Black Belt* magazine was published every other month and each issue contained a favorite fighting techniques section in it. That is where I learned the first of my competitive fighting moves. After I began to travel to tournaments. I asked questions of any black belt who would hold still. I pestered everybody and anyone for information until I became a regional, and later, national fighting champion. I became known as "Super Dan".

Those are just a few of the reasons why I am qualified to write this book. I had to basically figure a lot of it by myself. Yes, I did attend classes and trained at the school I was raised in and that was invaluable. But the bulk of my present day knowledge came from very exacting and extensive research. Enough about me. Let's move on to what you are going to get out of this book.

Baking a cake...

With this book you are baking a cake. What do I mean by that? I will give you the ingredients, but you are going to have to mix them up and put them into the oven to bake your own cake. You are going to have to figure which concepts apply or appeal to you the best. You're going to have to do the drills yourself. You are going to bake your own cake. This contains my ingredients for baking the best cake you can bake. You have to bake it yourself. Study the ingredients. Use a dictionary liberally. Understand the concepts. Test them out. Don't take my word for anything just because I'm Super Dan. Make them your own. Work what works best for you. Bake your own cake. And have fun doing it.

This book is based on three elements:

* Perception,

* Movement, and

* How to employ that movement.

I go more into this topic later on page 27 of this book, but the three above elements are the bottom line foundation points of the Super Dan Method of Free-Fighting. I look at, at the age of 65, what can I do. I can perceive. I can move. I have strategies to employ how I can move. I am no longer the multi-kicking speed

1

that I was in my 20s and early 30s. The physical attributes I once had, have diminished. Okay, I knew that was going to happen, but I have one thing in my favor. I have studied free-fighting to a point to where there is nothing mysterious about it at all. Nothing. The Super Dan Method is based on that understanding. Read on.

This book is broken down into several parts. There is the history of karate free-fighting and how it has changed over the years. Then there are the three major elements of the Super Dan Method: perception, motion, and how to employ that motion. The first section of the book deals with how I subdivide how one perceives. This is really the meat and potatoes of how I look at free-fighting and are elements that will raise your own free-sparring and free-fighting abilities for the long term. The second section of this book deals with how you bring the white belt into free-sparring and develop them so that they are not afraid of getting into the next step, free-fighting. Section three of the book delineates the major strategies I have used over the years. A key point that I have stressed in every book since my first one, *American Freestyle Karate – A Guide to Sparring*, is to take what works for you and make it yours. None of this is gospel unless you are a student in my school. Otherwise pick and choose according to your experience and mindset.

Note: I shot a DVD video in conjunction with this book which is available at my website *wwwdanandersonbooksndvds.com*. All of the stills in this book are taken from that video footage. Hence, there are pictures of me demonstrating techniques with my mouth open. In the video, I am describing what I am doing. I never free-spar or free-fight with my mouth open. That is a good way to accidentally get your jaw broken. Please, don't emulate the stills in that manner. Keep your mouth closed while sparring or free-fighting.

How this book came about…

In the fall of 2016, I began a personal project that really had its beginnings five years prior. I took a physical test for my 9th degree black belt. I had done the first three sections of the test; basics, kata and self-defense. Last up was free-fighting. My first partner was Jason Wegley. I was pretty bushed by then so I wasn't going to get into a stand-still slug fest, even if I was in Texas. So I moved like in the old days, circling, sticking and moving much like a point fighter. Afterwards, Linda Denley said to me in surprise, *"Look at*

Free-sparring during my 9th Dan test

you out there. Bouncing around like a teenager." My next sparring partner was Ray McCallum. This was a bit more stand-still, not a whole lot of dancing around. My third fight was Garrett Lee. The sparring in the test went well but in all three matches, something was a little wrong. I could not put my finger on it so I chalked it up to being very tired by that time.

Fast forward another five years and I decided to undergo a very personal project. You see, I would spar with my students and I could pull off a number of the old tricks, but I was missing something. I was missing the youthful attributes of flexibility and raw speed. Back in the ancient days, I was known for my kicking abilities among other things. I could kick head height several times without putting my foot down to the floor. I was 25-30 years old then. I am 64 years old at the time of this writing. My hips won't do that anymore so I made a decision. I would acknowledge what I couldn't do anymore, as well as acknowledge what I CAN do, and attempt to "re-hard wire the system" – change my free-fighting from Super Dan flash to a solid fighting base.

The results were terrific. I settled down and worked on five basic principles (fully delineated later in this book as the Five Pillars), honed the skills, and then finally put them to the test. I decided to enter a tournament to see if I could maintain what I worked on under pressure. To make something clear, I am not a big fan of tournaments these days. I long overstayed my welcome and when I was done with them, I was really done with them. So why did I chose a tournament to check out the skills? Well, I knew my students so well that sparring them was not a true test. I raised them up from their first day on the training floor. I know what they are going to do a week before they do it. That's not quite what I call a test. A tournament where someone is trying to beat me is a test. There was one catch, however. As a former national and world champion, competing in my age bracket, to me, was not enough of a test. I needed to have my feet put to the fire, so in addition to competing in the 50 years and up division, I competed in the 18-34 years old division as well.

An old buzzard against the young guns. This was my idea of a test! I won my age division and took 4th in the 18-34 division and you know what? I acquitted myself very well and really sorted out what really is the Super Dan Method of Free-fighting. That is what this book is all about. It began as an experiment in senior's sparring and fleshed out to sorting out the underlying principles I rely on and those same principles can be applied to any fighter who wants to make his or her skills advance to the next level. Read on.

March 2017 competition

Introduction...

"'American Freestyle Karate' is the name tag I give to my method of instruction in order to convey the idea of a non-Oriental type of karate. Rather than the idea of a set style to be passed on from master to senior student, I like my studio and method of karate to that of a boxing gym headed by a particular trainer (e.g. Muhammad Ali's camp headed by Angelo Dundee of Floyd Patterson's camp headed by Cus D'Amato). Not exactly the way traditional karate is looked at, but then again, this is not a very traditional style."

I wrote that over 38 years ago. It was pretty revolutionary at the time. It was breaking from the usual karate mold of this or that style of karate to a more personal approach. Today it is a commonplace concept. So, what is the Super Dan Method of Free-fighting? It is the result of my research in that area, free-fighting, boiled down to the essentials that will make anyone better at it. Free-fighting is no mystery to me and has not been for many years. I have researched the heck out of this topic beginning back to when I was a white belt. It was an activity I specialized in for quite some time. I've always had a motto: "If I can do it, anybody can." Let's go back to my roots.

My karate career began on November 18, 1966 in Vancouver, Washington. I was raised up in a town of 24,000 people. There was no established karate school in all of Vancouver, Washington. I began my lessons at the Marshall Recreation Center at the age of 14. There were no good movies, no instructional books, no internet, no YouTube. There was my teacher, Loren Christensen, *Black Belt* magazine, and Bruce Lee co-starring in the television program "The Green Hornet". That's it. There was one more thing – an insatiable desire to learn.

 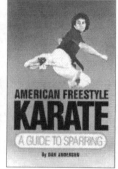 

Loren Christensen (1969)   American Freestyle Karate   Mike Engeln (R—1969)

As a kid, I would read about tournament fighters like Chuck Norris, Joe Lewis, Allan Steen and many others. They became my heroes. *Black Belt* magazine and later on, *Karate Illustrated* would do feature articles on these fighters. My favorite parts of the articles were photo demonstrations of their favorite fighting techniques. I ate those up like ice cream. My research began there. I would digest what they did and try them out in the class. I remember very clearly learning the Chuck Norris move of faking a backhand chop (knife-hand strike) and then doing a spinning back kick. We had done nothing like this in class so I drilled it at home until I could do it without falling over. I demonstrated it to Loren and asked him if this was the correct way of doing the spinning back kick. He suppressed the look of *"What the heck is he doing?"* and told me it was "something like that". Years later, I could tell from his reaction that he had never seen it before. The research continued. I learned the spinning back kick from an article on Chuck Norris. I learned how to double kick from an article on John Natividad. I learned how to fake a back fist to open my opponent up for a follow up side kick to the ribs from an article on Joe Lewis. As an under belt, I would take voluminous notes and make drawings. Anything to learn and add to my knowledge. I competed in my first tournament, at age 15, in the white belt division. I lost my first match but something rare happened. Instead of being dejected, I got bit by the bug. Instead of wanting to quit, I wanted to excel. I wanted to be a champion. I went to every tournament I could. I fought everywhere.

Allen Steen *Joe Lewis & Chuck Norris* *John Natividad*

When I began to compete on the national circuit, I took on the attribute of the fly on the wall. I hung around the better fighters, kept my mouth shut, and listened. Now and again, I would ask a question and listen very carefully to the answer. I would take very good mental notes and go home and drill. I learned how to do the "California Blitz" by watching Howard Jackson. I learned how to deliver a side kick, bypassing the traditional chamber, by watching Jeff Smith coach another. I learned about training myself to be ambidextrous by reading Chuck Norris articles and working with Demetrius Havanis. I watched, listened, and learned. The research continued. By 1974, I was consistently rated in the Top 20 karate fighters in the US. By this time, I could watch and pick up fighters favorite or dominant moves and how they did them. Howard Jackson's blitz was a combination of his lead hand activating while his rear leg pushed off. It was a simultaneous move. Frank Smith and Tonny Tulleners were perpetual motion machines. Each kick and punch was smoothly meshed together in one complete flowing motion with no hesitations or gaps in their movements. Bill Wallace picked up his left knee so high that it guarded his head against his opponent's counter punch. His kicking foot was in a direct line with his opponent and it was in a side kick preparatory position. From here he would do one of three kicks, the side kick, round kick or the hook kick.

Jeff Smith (L) *Howard Jackson (L)* *Frank Smith (R)* *Bill Wallace*

I watched them all. The instructor I got my black belt from, Bruce Terrill, inspired me to look at karate scientifically. He was not a believer in the "secrets of the arts". Everything had a logical explanation. He was influenced by Bruce Lee's first senior student, Taky Kimura, back in the 1960s and taught his curriculum in that manner. He steered me away from the "magical mystery tour" that is prevalent in martial arts and toward the practical. By the time I left him in 1975, I was ready to continue my research on my own…and I did.

By 1979, I was one of the best karate fighters in America. I was in the Top Ten. My study continued. I studied the leading fighters of the day: Keith Vitali, Ray McCallum, Steve Fisher, Larry Kelly, Jimmy Tabares, Mike Genova, and many others. They were my opponents now and I learned their strengths and weaknesses. My book, *American Freestyle Karate: A Guide To Sparring* was written during this time.

Keith Vitali, me, Ray McCallum, Herb Johnson, John Longstreet, Mike Genova, Larry Kelly - 1979 Mid-America Diamond Nationals.

In 1983, I began competing in the Amateur Athletic Union (AAU) circuit which used Japanese rules. What was called for a point was drastically different than what was called in the American point game. I studied and adapted and did fairly well. I was made a member of the US team after winning the silver and bronze medals in the 1984 AAU championships. My excursion in this kind of competition culminated in winning two gold medals at the 1990 Seattle Goodwill Games and a world championship at the Funakoshi Shotokan Karate Association World Championships in 2002. The research continued.

1990 Seattle Goodwill Games   *2002 Funakoshi Shotokan Karate Assn World Championships*

I was one of the first Americans to form a completely American system of karate in 1978. I wrote the first comprehensive book on free-fighting in 1979, American Freestyle Karate: A Guide To Sparring. I became a national and world champion, as well as a Goodwill Games double gold medalist in free-fighting. I have taught seminars all over the world on this subject and others. This was followed up three years later with being awarded my 9th degree black belt in Modern Arnis (Filipino martial arts). I am one of a handful to be awarded the prestigious Joe Lewis Eternal Warrior Award. On May 13, 2017, I was awarded my 10th dan in karate. On the overall whole, that's not too bad for a kid who began martial arts 1,000 miles from any famous karate dojo and had to basically pull himself up by the bootstraps.

Presentation during the 10th Dan ceremony.   *Awarded my 10th Dan certificate.*

It has been many years since I have competed but the research continued on. My motto is *"If I can do it, anyone can".* This was recently put to the test with yet another research project I undertook. Like I said before, at the time of this writing I am 64 years old. The young, spry kid of yesteryear has since long vanished. Now and again I will see a video of a match up on Facebook or on YouTube and wonder *"Was I really that quick?"* My wife once remarked how flexible I was back in those days. The research project was this: I am no longer 25 years old. Can I "re-hardwire the system" of how I spar? I hadn't done any sparring training, actual training, since 2002 when I won a world championship in my age bracket. I got to work and found that I could. Originally, this book was going to be one on sparring for seniors. Yes, really. Sparring for seniors. When I looked at the principles, concepts and techniques involved, I realized what I had on my hands was the "Super Dan Method of Free-fighting" ready to be delineated.

Section One:

History of the Development of Karate Free-Fighting

What Is Sparring/Free-Fighting...

The first thing you will find out about me is that I am big on having the correct definitions, so let's define some terms right away. Here are several definitions of the word "spar":

- Make the motions of boxing without landing heavy blows, as a form of training
- (Boxing) to make the motions of attack and defense with the arms and fists, especially as a part of training
- To fight with an opponent in a short bout or practice session, as in boxing or the martial arts

"Sparring partner":

- (Boxing) a person who practices with a boxer during training
- Someone who helps a boxer practice, someone who a boxer spars with for training

Note the use of the words "practice", "helps", and "training". Sparring is a cooperative effort. Sparring is not fighting. Let's look at the definition of the word "fight".

- Take part in a violent struggle involving the use of physical blows or the use of weapons
- A battle or combat
- To engage in battle or single combat; attempt to defend oneself against or subdue, defeat, or destroy an adversary

Sparring is practicing. Fighting is about winning. Sparring is training, leading one to learn how to fight. Sparring is a cooperative effort in learning those skills. Sparring, in the beginning, is extremely cooperative. There should be no winner or loser. What I have seen over and over again in different schools of karate is there is an inadvertent blend of sparring and fighting. The sparring becomes a covert game of fighting, a game of one-upsmanship. I had been a prime example of it in my younger years. Many times my sparring sessions were a game of me beating on my partner. It was a great ego boost...for me. I'm sure my partner did not feel the same way.

I remember reading about boxers who lost their edge in what was called "gym wars". The sparring sessions turned into battles in the ring. The fighters would spend all of their hard won skills during training and left nothing remaining for the fight they were training for. The opposite of that was Muhammad Ali. His sparring sessions looked unremarkable.

He worked on skills to be used in the ring. A perfect example of that is when he trained for the first fight with the heavyweight champion, Sonny Liston. Liston was a menacing character with knockout power in both fists. The prevailing opinion was that Liston would catch up with Ali and destroy him. Ali had a sparring partner named "Shotgun" Sheldon. He would let Sheldon corner him on the ropes and pound away at him. He didn't dance or use his famous snake-licker jab or his amazing speed. He would lie on the ropes and let Sheldon

pound away at him and work on ways of covering up against the blows. What was he doing? He was training for the possibility of Liston cornering him in the same fashion. He was training for "just in case..." Well, that never happened in that particular fight, but many years down the road that training came in useful against another fighter who patterned himself after Liston, George Foreman. Ali spent a lot of that fight laying back on the ropes letting Foreman tire himself out by wasting punches that

never landed. Ali ended up winning by a knockout.

The point of this story is that this is a perfect example of sparring being training. Ali didn't work on what he was skilled at. He worked on what he needed to become skilled at. Then, he could use it in a fight if he needed to. This is the viewpoint I take for the Super Dan Method of Free-Fighting. In learning free-fighting, one must first learn to free-spar, and prior to that one learns to spar cooperatively.

Orientation…

Before I get into the different types of free-fighting there is something I want to clarify and simplify at the same time. All free-fighting types, styles, or methods boil down to one thing – orientation.

Fighting is one of the most perfect examples of unbridled chaos there is. Fighting contains all kinds of elements to it that will throw your composure right out the door. It has wild emotions, high-speed random motion from potentially all angles, and best of all it contains pain, punishment, injury and possibly death. How's that for chaos! It's like putting 6 cats in a box and turning on the blender. It's wild at its mildest.

Any method of handling that chaos gives you an orientation from which to operate from.

Popular martial arts such as Shotokan karate, Taekwondo, Wing chun kung fu, Thai boxing, Judo, Brazilian Jiu-Jitsu, Silat, Arnis/Eskrima are all orientation points. The Bill "Superfoot" Wallace System, Joe Lewis Fighting System, the Super Dan Method of Free-fighting are all orientation points. The styles and systems and methods all stave off or handle the confusion of the chaos that is called fighting. All too often you will get someone who will state an absolute such as *"95% of all fights go to the ground."* Why is this? Because this is the orientation point of the speaker. A hard core striker might counter that with, *"That's right. 95% of all fights go to the ground. One hard punch and yes, you will go to the ground…courtesy of me."* Well, that's his orientation point. When you get into a competition match, it comes down to who can keep his own orientation point and cause their opponent to lose theirs. As my student, Tim Gustavson says, *"it's who can impose their will on the other decides the game."* That's a military definition of war – imposing policy on another. Training in these orientation points is called free-fighting and depending on what kind of orientation you are trained in or prefer is the kind of free-fighting you'll use. So what are they?

Different types of free-fighting…

Just as there are different kinds of kicks and punches you can use in striker based free-fighting, there are different kinds of ways to free-fight. I'll briefly delineate a few of them. Free-fighting is limiting fighting (or combat fighting) using an agreed upon set of rules. This is either competitive freestyle or fight training in a school. There are all sorts of competitive fighting:

- Point fighting is where you stop and acknowledge (in some form or manner) the fact that one of the players got hit. Whoever gets in the hit or kick first scores the point. Then the match continues until you get the amount of points needed to win or if you're ahead when the time period runs out.

- Continuous point fighting (karate) is run more like a boxing match where the fighters engage for a certain time limit and for a certain number of rounds. The action does not stop if one of the players gets hit. They may continue hitting and/or defending or they may back off and look for a different opening or whatever. The key difference is there is no official stop in the action. In America, they wear a helmet, covering over the hands and feet, and control their strikes. Points can be tallied as the competitors fight or rounds can be awarded.

- There is a continuous type of free-fighting in Japan (kyokushin) where it is full contact, yet has the proviso that you cannot punch to the face. These fighters use no protective covering at all.

- It is the same with taekwondo free-sparring. Olympic taekwondo is more of a kicking oriented combat game in which the players wear headgear and body pads. Points are awarded for kicks and punches that score with power. A match can be ended by a knock out. Kicks are allowed to the head, but punches are not. Taekwondo generally sparring relies on kicking to do all the scoring and tends to stop the action if the players get within hand range. They will tend to either try to kick the other player, if in hand range, or push them off to get distance for kicking. Taekwondo players wear a chest protector and a close fitting helmet during their sparring and competition.

- Kickboxing or full-contact karate is a karate adaptation of boxing where the fighters wear boxing gloves and, at times, foot pads of some sort. The matches go by rounds of 2-3 minutes in length. Targeting is generally above the waist of your opponent. You can, however, either kick the thighs of your opponent or not, depending on which association you fight for. The rounds are scored as in boxing.

- Thai boxing expands on kickboxing where you use knee and elbow strikes as well as kicks to the thigh and lower legs. No pads of any sort are worn except for boxing gloves. Thai boxing/Japanese kick-boxing is a rougher version of American kickboxing. San Shou/San Da is Chinese kickboxing that allows the addition of throwing techniques to the above techniques of Thai & Japanese kickboxing techniques.

- "Mixed martial arts" (MMA) or cage fighting is a combination of kicking, striking and grappling where you work to defeat your opponent by knock out (by way of striking or choking into unconsciousness), by submission (causing the opponent to give up the match) or by decision of the judges.

These are overviews and there are variations on each of these types. These are all forms of free-fighting. Yes, you are going for the win, yet you are governed by rules. There are certain things you cannot do. Yes, you can get hurt doing this but, at the same time, it can be stopped by an official. This could be considered as sport combat or game fight. I do not mean this as any kind of slight but to define it for what it is. I played the competition game for many years and I got very good at it. I do not believe for a moment that it is real deal combat. Fight training in a school is also limited by the degree of contact one can make and by the degree of injury one can dish out and take. This is about as close to fighting as you can safely get.

History of karate free-fighting...

A history of free-fighting could take a multi-volume set of books if it were inclusive and historically precise. For the purpose of this book, I am taking a look as how karate free-fighting developed from the original karate of Okinawa through to the present time in the United States.

Anko Itosu

Free-fighting, or kumite (free hands in Japanese) was not a part of karate in Okinawa in the early days. Training in Okinawa consisted of careful training in basics, partner exercises, kata (prearranged solo exercises) and supplementary weight and implement training. Karate was a fairly secretive affair at that time.

In the early 1900s, Yasutsune "Anko" Itosu introduced karate training to the middle schools. Japan was undergoing a change from the isolationist nation that it was to becoming part of the world. In doing so, the caste system was abolished which meant the end of the samurai class. The wearing of the twin swords that symbolized their status (as well as their sanctioned indiscriminate use) was abolished. In essence, Japan chilled out.

Okinawa, which was ruled by Japan for the last 400 years, was being accepted as somewhat like a county in the far corner of Wyoming, part of the country but nothing much of any consequence in their eyes. Bear in mind that in the previous 400 years the Japanese overlords banned the ownership of weapons by any Okinawan citizen. The only people who were permitted weapons of any kind were the samurai. Therefore karate training was held in secret, behind closed doors and often at night, away from any prying eyes of the Japanese occupation forces.

Aside from opening up is shores for world trade, Japan was building up its military force. Okinawa saw that karate training was a good way for the youth of Okinawa to build up strong young men who would be able to fit in with the Japanese military. Karate training became public. In around 1917, Crown Prince Hirohito was given a demonstration of the art of karate in Okinawa. Those in the Japanese delegation who attended were enthralled by the demonstration. Karate was beginning to be recognized as something new. Following that successful presentation, a number of the masters got together to hand pick the teacher who would go to Japan to begin to spread their art. They picked a middle aged school teacher, Gichin Funakoshi, to be the one.

Funakoshi was neither the best martial artist in Okinawa nor was he the best fighter. He was the best educated, however, and was a perfect pick to present their art. Humble, but with a fierce dedication, Funakoshi set out to popularize their native fighting art in Japan. *Harry Cook's book, Shotokan Karate: A Precise History*, covers this bit of history very well.

An interesting point to make is that in his presentation of karate on the Japanese mainland, he only taught basics, kata, and pre-arranged one and three step sparring (strictly formalized one punch or three punch attacks that were defended against and then countered). There was no free play or unrehearsed combat training.

The following is a quote from Randall Hassell's book *Shotokan Karate – Its' History & Evolution* (www.TamashiiPress.com). Master Masatoshi Nakayama told him:

"My seniors...knew only kata; it was the only thing Master Funakoshi taught them. But in my generation, things began to change. The people in my generation were required to study martial arts beginning in grammar school,

Gichin Funakoshi

and continuing all the way through graduation from high school. Karate was not taught in the schools at the time, so all of us had studied judo or kendo. But judo and kendo were centered on combat – throwing an opponent or actually striking an opponent with a sword. So, the idea of combat was deeply ingrained in us, and we really needed the combative aspect that karate lacked. Master Funakoshi understood this, and he began to change his teaching methods to meet the needs of our younger generation. We needed more than just kata all the time, and he realized that things would have to change if he was going to attract young people and see his art grow."

Masatoshi Nakayama

In another camp, that of Gogen Yamaguchi and his Goju-ryu students, another rough form of free-fighting was beginning to take place. From an interview by Graham Noble:

"Gosei, Yamaguchi's eldest son, said that when his father started jyu-kumite practice in the 1930s, 'Other schools thought it was 'street fighting' and wouldn't spar with them... My father started free fighting when all the other styles stayed with the traditional workouts. In the Goju style my father wanted it to be more practical. He invented his own way of working out. You used your head, elbow, anything. You used what was effective." And in his 1998 book on Goju-kumite, Goshi Yamaguchi wrote of this early time that "It was referred to as 'jissen kumite' (actual fighting sparring). Therefore such dangerous techniques as tori-waza, (grappling techniques), gyaku-te waza (twisting techniques), and shime-waza (choking techniques) were used, which resulted in many injuries.' "

At around the same time in Okinawa, the founder of Goju-ryu karate, Chojun Miyagi, began experimenting with free-fighting with protective armor. From the same interview: In the December 1989 number of his IOGKF newsletters Morio Higaonna added this information:

"It was about this time, for a period of one year between 1929 and 1930, that Miyagi Sensei PIC began experimenting with Iri-Kumi (free sparring) using protective equipment. He ordered the protective equipment, head guards, chest guards, groin guards and fist protectors, from Osaka, mainland Japan. For the most part it was high school boys who practiced the Iri-Kumi. Punches and kicks were delivered with full speed and power with no consideration for control or for limiting dangerous techniques. The fighting that took place could at best be described as rough. Miyagi Sensei's idea was not to practice Iri-Kumi as a sport, but rather to research the possibilities of realistic free sparring with protective equipment. After 1 year of Iri-Kumi training the spirited fighting of the high school boys had resulted in a high level of injuries, particularly to the neck and toes. The neck, because of the heavy head guard (which had a heavy metal grill to protect the face) which created a whiplash effect on the neck when the head was struck, and the toes, due to the metal grill on the head guard and also because of the chest guard which was a solid design similar to kendo armour.

"Because of the high incidence of injury due to the unsuitable design of the protective equipment, Miyagi Sensei stopped this type of training. He decided that for the majority of students at least, as far as kumite training was concerned, it was better to concentrate on yakusoku kumite (prearranged sparring), san dan uke harai (basic attack and block training) and kakie (push hands training). This type of training he decided was most important".

Chojun Miyagi

Morio Higaonna

15

At this point, free-fighting was exactly that, free fighting, and the point was to beat the hell out of your partner and dominate him completely. This was completely in line with the viewpoint of Japanese fighting spirit. What has been documented is that there were two groups who engaged in this early form of free-fighting development, the Shotokan group and Gogen Yamaguchi's Goju-ryu. This excerpt from Graham Noble's interview with Gosei Yamaguchi shows how the two groups developed their distinct fighting methods. (This interview took place at Potter's Leisure Resort, near Great Yarmouth. 14 July 2008, IKGA European Gasshaku [special training] and was posted on the website Hawaii Karate Seinenkai)

Graham Noble: - and they all said that the Goju fighters were very tough.
Gosei Yamaguchi: Oh yes, because at that time there was no karate competition (tournaments), so my father had many good friends in martial arts, so the Asakusa dojo had good connections with other groups, I remember when they would spar, so, oh sometimes very dangerous training.

Gosei Yamaguchi

GN: Did people sometimes get hurt?
GY: Yes, breaks (broken arms, noses etc) sometimes. At that time Goju had a good connection with the Shotokan group. Ritsumeikan University in Kyoto had had a good connection with Takushoku University. Kanazawa sensei and many others graduated from Takushoku University, so still we had a good connection with Shotokan and Nakayama sensei. And my oldest brother, he went to Takushoku University.

GN: The Shotokan people and the Wado people said the Goju students were very difficult to fight because they would use techniques like haito (ridge hand) and kin geri (groin kick), and they would fight close in.
GY: Yes, very close. Now people all fight similar, but at that time Goju used to use cat stance, neko ashi, and Shotokan would use a big stance and take a long distance (to fight). So this is something funny, Goju like to come in close and Shotokan like to keep a long distance. I saw many fighting injuries.

GN: So the fighting was hard?
GY: Yes, we did very hard training but afterwards, when we finish, good friendships.

GN: When they fought Wado-ryu and Shotokan people, how did the Goju fighters get in on them, because Shotokan is a long distance style?
GY: My father used cat stance, and so (inaudible) control the distance. Also we used many low kicks like groin kicks and knee joint kicks, while Shotokan people liked to do more dynamic kicks, so when they were coming close they could not use those kicks.

GN: Kase sensei and Kanazawa sensei also told me that the Goju people were good at throwing people down when they got close in.
GY: That's right, throwing techniques, and they would also do things like standing on the opponent's foot, so they couldn't move - very surprising."

Such were the beginnings of kumite, free-fighting, in Japan. In 1957, the Japan Karate Association (JKA - the group the Shotokan karate practitioners formed) decided to hold a tournament among themselves. This was the first All-Japan Karate Championships won by Hirokazu Kanazawa. An interesting note to make at this point is my researching and figuring out why the JKA school of karate fought with the stress being on delivering the rear leg front kick and straight punch as their primary types of attack to the exclusion of all else.

It baffled me for a long time. What I have found out is that the beginnings of this came out of Japanese military training in World War II. From Graham Noble's article, *Master Funakoshi's Karate, The History and Development of the Empty Hand Art Part III*:

"Taiji Kase, who trained at the Shotokan in the last year or so of the war, remembered that emphasis was placed on strong basics and intense practice of kumite (especially jiyu-ippon) with much physical contact. Kase, a person not given to exaggeration, described it as "very hard". Tatsuo Suzuki told me that the well-rounded pre-war training gave way to practice on "fighting", and he stressed "fighting" rather than sparring (jiyu-kumite). I had heard stories (without details) of Yoshitaka Funakoshi and Shigeru Egami teaching special troops during the war. I asked Harada sensei about this and he told me what he had heard.

Taiji Kase   *Yoshitaka Funakoshi & Shigeru Egami*

"The institution concerned was the Nakano School, a training school for military espionage analogous to our MI5. Trainees were on a one year course covering undercover work, guerrilla warfare and so on. Unarmed combat was also included and the original teacher for this was Morihei Uyeshiba (of Aikido). Uyeshiba himself was good but when the students tried to apply the techniques they couldn't make them work under real conditions. In a way, Aikido had too much "technique" for the limited one year of training. The military leaders decided to look at karate as an alternative, and they observed the different styles, such as Goju, Wado, and Shotokan.

Morihei Uyeshiba

"Goju-ryu, with its heavy stress on sanchin training, did not seem to have the practical application necessary, at least in its initial stages, and Wado-ryu technique seemed too "light". However, the Shotokan style as demonstrated by Yoshitaka (Funakoshi) looked impressive, and he was asked to teach at the Nakano School. Unfortunately, he was too ill and it was Shigeru Egami who did the actual teaching. Egami concentrated on two techniques: choku-zuki (straight punch) and mae-geri (front kick), and when he began teaching a class he would pick out participants and tell them to attack him as hard as they could. In this way he was able to prove the validity of his technique. Injuries were frequent. Kicks were often delivered to the shins - and this was while wearing boots.' "

This was the first point where free-fighting had to be performed in a certain way. It was karate based on combat efficiency being mass produced, so to speak. The emphasis was on front kick and straight punch. This is what could be taught quickly. This morphed into karate free-fighting and later into tournament competition in Japan. These two techniques became the basis for karate free-fighting and if you didn't do them in a tournament, it wouldn't gain you a point in the match. Herein lies the beginning of the influence tournament competition had in the development of free-fighting.

When karate was transplanted to the USA, the first tournaments were Japanese influenced with the "reverse punch" being the prevalent being called for a point. Note: a "reverse punch" is a mistranslation of the term gyaku tsuki – "opposite punch". The mistranslation caught on, however, and became a standard term. The reverse punch is analogous to a cross in boxing, a punch delivered with your rear hand. Front hand strikes such as a jab or a hook were not called for points because they were "not karate". They were boxing.

Kicks were delivered with the rear leg because of the power they could generate. If you wanted to successfully compete, these were the parameters you were stuck with. A key factor in early tournaments was that your strikes had to be delivered with enough power to, at the bare minimum, be able to stun or knock out your opponent if they landed with full force. There was no protective padding worn on the hands or feet and the contact was hard.

For the first 5-7 years, injuries were part of the game. It was not uncommon to draw blood with punches to the face or to knock the wind out of your opponent with a body punch. A very good example of the above was a match between Fred Wren and Chuck Norris at the US Karate Championships in Dallas, Texas, that (Norris student) Bob Barrow told me about. I believe the year was 1969. In one of the first exchanges Wren caught Norris with a punch to the nose, breaking it. Norris was given time to recover. Wren got the point. In the next two clashes Norris hit Wren to the body so hard that the first time he knocked the wind totally out of him and dropped him. The second time he hit him so hard in the body that he knocked Wren out. Norris got the point for both punches and was awarded a point each time. Norris won the match 2-1. This was how it was in Texas in 1969.

Fred Wren (R)

1970 saw the beginning of what was to be known as "the Johnson Rule". Pat Johnson, a student of Chuck Norris, and a very good competitor in his own right, instituted a "no face contact, no blood" rule in a tournament he promoted. The rule stated that if you drew blood from face contact you were immediately disqualified. This rule was adopted by many tournament promoters and soon became the norm for competition. You now had to control strikes to the face. The body was still open to hard contact and it varied from tournament to tournament exactly how hard you could hit there.

From 1964 to 1974 there was an unprecedented development in karate skills across the United States. This began with Chuck Norris competing in a Japanese style tournament and being beaten by Tonny Tulleners. Norris had trained in Korea in a style that emphasized kicking, Tang Soo Do. Tulleners smothered his kicks and beat him with punches. So what did Chuck Norris do? He did what is common place now but was unthinkable back in the 1960s. He cross-trained. He sought out Fumio Demura, Hidetaka Nishiyama, and Takiyuki Kubota and worked on developing his punching techniques and went on to become dominant in tournament competition.

Pat Johnson   Tonny Tulleners (R)   Tak Kubota   Hidetaka Nishiyama

Roughly from this point on, the development of free-fighting (in America if not the world) went from karate style-emphasis and dictates (such as how Shotokan players fight as opposed to Taekwondo or Kung Fu players fought) to the directions tournament competition were taking. This is an important point to make as, in many schools, karate free-fighting mostly resembles the tournament game being played in their area rather than skills that will help you in a self-defense situation. This holds true for each major division of Oriental striking arts, taekwondo, Japanese karate, kung fu, not just American karate.

With a combination of the "Johnson Rule" and the success of Chuck Norris' cross-training, free-fighting skills began a period of unprecedented development. Joe Lewis introduced the lead hand strike (both the back fist and front jab). Lewis was a heavyweight competitor who moved with the speed of a middleweight. He demonstrated how hard you could hit with the front hand and front leg (on several unfortunate opponents in the ring) and these were added to what could score. Skilled kickers such as Skipper Mullins from Texas, John Natividad from California, Michael Warren from New York, and Bill Wallace from Indiana began using their legs as adroitly as other fighters used their hands. This began the implementation of using double or triple kicks (kicking two or three times before setting the kicking leg down the floor) successfully in competition.

Skipper Mullins (R)

To add to this there were several other influences that affected free-fighting. The first of these was that Black Belt magazine began a Top Ten ratings system and published the results annually. Now, there was more incentive to compete. Tournament karate was never a big money sport, but instituting national recognition was something that appealed to the American competitor.

The popularity of Bruce Lee was another influence. Lee was in a television show called "The Green Hornet" and he played a role where he was the Kung Fu fighting chauffeur of the hero. His moves were crisp and dynamic and he looked authentic. In a two-part interview in Black Belt magazine he uttered martial arts blasphemy – that the practice of kata would not help you learn how to fight. This datum that you could not learn how to fight without practicing kata, was something that was preached incessantly by the teachers of Japanese karate to the American student. Well, here was an Oriental martial artist who said the complete opposite. This was taken and run with by many karate players in the US.

Bruce Lee

Free-fighting changed from the limited straight punch/front kick approach to one where any technique, as long as it could hit hard, could be used for competition. The targeting was pretty liberal. You could strike anywhere on the head and neck, to the body front and back, and to the groin (if you weren't wearing a protective cup, well, that was your fault). You could grab your opponent anywhere on his body, arm, leg, or jacket, to deliver your strikes. You could sweep your opponent's legs to take him to the floor and hit or kick him while he was on the ground. You would only be penalized if you didn't control his fall and he got injured when he hit the floor.

As far as scoring techniques, it was now open season. Techniques and counter-techniques were being developed weekly, as each fighter in the Top Ten ratings were working overtime to outdo each other in the next match.

In 1973, Jhoon Rhee developed the first free-fighting hand and foot pads to be used in American competition (pictured with Linda Denley). These were the Saf-T-Punch and Saf-T-Kick (™). They were developed so that one could make contact to the head with both kicks and punches. It took several years for them to catch on across the US, but catch on they did. Free-fighting changed again. Now contact was being made to the head and it was beginning to be easier for officials to call scoring points. The competitors' sense of distancing was becoming more acute as pulling punches to the head often resulted in them being ever so slightly out of range and actually missing the target.

Jhoon Rhee   *Linda Denley*

In 1974, with the advent of PKA (Professional Karate Association) full contact karate, a line in the sand was drawn. The PKA was the brainchild of Mike Anderson, a taekwondo black belt under Allen Steen from Texas. It combined karate kicks and punches with the rules of boxing whereby one could win by outpointing your opponent or knocking him out. Anderson, along with financial backers Don and Judy Quine, scored a major coup when he arranged for ABC's Wide World of Sports to televise the first world championships on television. Karate was shown only one time before on that program in 1964 where Mike Stone PIC knocked out his opponent in a point fighting match. ABC declared that it was too violent to be shown on television. In 1974, the four major point fighters Joe Lewis, Jeff Smith, Bill Wallace and Howard Jackson for world titles.

The game changes...

With the PKA garnering national attention, the bulk of rated point fighters left the point game to test their fortunes in the full contact game. The point game began its slow shift from a strong game of free-fighting to more and more of a game of tag. And once again free-fighting in America followed suit. Tournaments began to change the rules in an effort to make point karate more spectator friendly. Kicks to the groin were the first tactics to go. This was followed by no striking the back of the head or spine. Then takedowns became illegal. From there you could get two points for a kick to the head instead of the usual one. You would no longer be penalized for running out of the ring or dropping to the floor to avoid an attack. By the mid-1980s points were given for speedy techniques which touched the target regardless of the power they were delivered with. The game shifted more and more in the direction of "karate-tag". And it continued in this path for decades.

Bill Wallace, Jeff Smith and Joe Lewis after winning the PKA World Championships.

On November 12, 1993, there was a televised event that shook the karate world. The first Ultimate Fighting Championships (UFC) was broadcast to a pay per view audience. The UFC was the brainchild of Rorion Gracie from Brazil. A number of different fighters from varying disciplines came to fight it out in an elimination tournament. The rules were very simple. The only tactics that were prohibited were eye gouging and fish-hooking (putting a finger in your opponent's mouth and pulling). The objective was equally simple. You fight your opponent and either knock him out (by strikes or chokes) or cause him to submit (give up signified by tapping the mat or your opponent). It was an organized street brawl with a referee. This one event changed and shifted the course of martial arts across the world. A fighter found out what worked and what didn't. Grappling, which had been shunned by many, many karate fighters (myself included) was shown to be extremely effective against fighters who only kicked and punched. This brought on a new kind of free-fighting which included punching, kicking, takedowns, grappling, arm locks and chokes. This new sport was not for everyone but it became an outlet for those who wished to train harder and make stronger contact.

Taekwondo...

(Note: I include Taekwondo free-fighting because of the influence Japanese karate had in its formation as well as there were many Taekwondo/tangsoodo style players who competed in American karate competition.) The evolution of Korean Taekwondo free-fighting is not strongly documented. There are, however, several points in the evolution of it that are broadly known. Taekwondo was the brainchild of General Choi Hong Hi. In pre-WWII Korea it was fashionable for Korean families to send their children to Japan to go to university there. Choi Hong Hi was one of those who went to Japan for university training. It was there where he

General Choi Hong Hi

trained in Shotokan karate and earned a 2nd degree black belt. Taekwondo history is thoroughly documented in Alex Gillis' book, *A Killing Art: The Untold History of Taekwondo*, page 22:

"Choi practiced diligently in Japan, keeping the wrestler in mind, and within two years obtained a first-degree black belt. He stayed in Japan for four years... At the age of twenty-four, however, after finishing middle school and gaining a second-degree black belt...he returned to the village."

Choi returned to Korea and decided that Korea needed its own martial art and this eventually became Taekwondo. The Taekwondo that General Choi developed emphasized kicking far more than punching, even to the point where it was considered an insult to punch someone in the face but totally okay to kick someone there. Taekwondo instructors immigrated to the United States with notable instructors as Richard Chun, Ki Whang Kim, S. Henry Cho relocating in New York City and Jhoon Rhee and David Moon in Dallas, Texas.

Richard Chun   *Ki Whang Kim*   *S. Henry Cho*   *David Moon*

The fighters they turned out were powerful fighters and strong kickers. Texas Taekwondo fighters were especially fierce. I remember my instructor, Loren Christensen, telling me something interesting when I was a young under belt. Loren went into the armed forces in 1968 or thereabouts. He ended up being stationed in Vietnam as a military policeman in Saigon. He told me that there was only one group that the Viet Cong were afraid of – the ROK (Republic of Korea) Tigers. I remember reading a feature article on the ROK Tigers training in an issue of Black Belt magazine. This was very serious taekwondo training meant to be used on the battlefield. This runs parallel to how the Japanese infantry trained for World War II – no nonsense training for man to man combat. This is the Taekwondo that was brought to Texas by former Korean army captain, Jhoon Go Rhee. It was this hard core training that Allen Steen underwent and spread throughout the Lone Star state.

Jhoon Rhee

In the 1970s, Taekwondo was a full-contact game that allowed full power kicks to the head and body with head punches being disallowed. I fought in several of their tournaments and it was rugged. The only protection allowed was a torso protector (with a helmet being optional). Everything was bare fist and foot. The champions were strong fighters. The first American World Champion in Taekwondo came from the women's division. Marcia Hall of California won her division two years back to back (1979 & 1980). In 1988 Taekwondo was admitted into the Olympic Games in Seoul, Korea as an exhibition sport. Taekwondo was already popular around the world but this helped boost it in popularity even more but something was amiss. As it had been done with American point karate, Taekwondo rules were changing to a point were in the 2016 Olympics, former Olympic champion Herb Perez was comparing it to modern day point karate. All the fight went out of it and what was left was a game of foot tag.

Marcia Hall (L)   *Arlene Limas (R) 1988 Olympics*   *Me (R) in Taekwondo competition*

Japanese karate...

And what about where it began - Japanese style competition? I fought in the Japanese rules AAU karate tournaments in 1983 and 1984 and briefly reprised my role in it in the 1990 Seattle Goodwill Games. One of the things I liked about it was that you had to be very clean with your technique and had to have power in your shots in order to score. Good, solid points were the order of the day. It was a bit of a throwback to what I had learned back in the 1960s-early 1970s. Over the years, it has also become a game of tag where the punches are fully extended (meaning they touch instead of make an impact) and you now can score with head kicks and so on. Just as in American point karate and current day Taekwondo, the athletes are amazing but most of the actual "fight" is out of the game as currently played.

The point is...

Why am I making a fuss about the history of free-fighting? It is to show the history of the development of free-fighting (as taught in many schools) follows the path of martial arts tournaments. No more, no less. Free-fighting started out as a rugged mock-fighting or testing of skills and has developed into a fighting-esque preparation to a game of tag which is less related to self-defense than it ever has been. Targets that were once plentiful have now dwindled down to precious few. Tactics that embraced practitioners of any body type are now slanted to the young, long-limbed, and limber. Free-fighting, in karate, is now a specialized sort of activity that is exclusive, rather than inclusive. (That being said, there are schools who do not follow the "game of tag" approach to free-fighting training but go the opposite way. The Kyokushin school is a very good example. It has a rugged, full contact kind of free-fighting that is a very arduous affair. Certain kung fu schools train in San Shou/San Da full contact free-fighting.) My own personal emphasis lies in the all-inclusive approach. Training-wise, I reside in the middle ground, neither full-contact nor game of tag. I value strong free-fighting with an element of safety.

The Super Dan Method of Free Fighting...

So what is the Super Dan Method of Free-fighting? Well, let me tell you first what it is not. The Super Dan method is neither "body type specific" nor is it "attribute reliant". This means that anyone of any size or shape or age can use it and does not rely on youthful attributes such as speed or flexibility to make it work. Competition karate these days favors the long and lean body type. The better your reach is and the more limber you are, the better advantage you have over others.

The Super Dan Method is not that. It is a method or orientation to fighting which utilizes principles that govern all fighting and strategies and tactics that play to your own personal strengths. When I listen to senior students about their sparring abilities, too much sparring for seniors deals with "what I can't do anymore". That is a wrong emphasis. My emphasis is "what can you do?" That is the emphasis point. What can you *do*?

Well, the first thing you can do is you can *observe*. Learning how to understand and read what you observe is something that can be learned in the Super Dan Method of Free-Fighting.

The second thing you can do is that you can *move*. Knowing how you can move and how you can make that movement better is something that can be learned in the Super Dan Method of Free-Fighting.

The Super Dan Method of Free-fighting has morphed from what I could do back when I was young into what anyone can do effectively, no matter their age. The Super Dan Method of Free-fighting will benefit any student of any age, rank, and skill level and will take you to the next level. It is for you. If I can do it, anyone can.

I researched the heck out of the subject so that I could excel in it. I never considered that I had exceptional talent. I always considered that I had exceptional motivation to learn and research. That was my strength. My other strength was the ability to break things down and communicate them in a manner in which they could be easily understood. No fancy physics and scientific terms. Just plain English.

When I began my school in 1985, I knew it was time to transmit my knowledge to others. I always had the viewpoint that if I could do it, anybody can. The rub was that they had to understand it the way I did. That began an ongoing research project into how I did what I did and how to explain it so that someone else could duplicate it. I've written over 20 martial arts books and produced over 25 videos on the subject as part of that research.

I have reduced the Super Dan Method of Free-fighting down to five basic principles which I call:

The Five Pillars.

Section Two:

Perception

The Five Pillars to the Super Dan Method of Free-Fighting

It all begins with motion and perception...

I began a project in the fall of 2016, and it had to do with re-hardwiring my personal free-fighting. After my competitive years, I had let go many of the training habits I used many years as a youth. I cut back on my stretching, my free-fighting sessions, my kicking repetitions, the works - until I wasn't doing any training in karate.

I continued to train in Filipino Martial Arts, but as I got older, the explosive take-off, the speedy kicks, and limberness of youth faded. I was using my experience when I sparred my students (not to mention my seniority with them) and that was all fine and dandy. There were, however, good nights where I could do no wrong and bad nights where I felt like I was a white belt again. I was, in effect, relying on "past excesses". This is a term I picked up from Olympic swimming gold medalist Don Schollander. It has to do with relying on past training instead of working on current training skills. So, at my age (64 years old - when fighters have hung up their gloves long before then) what could I do?

Well, first, I could *perceive*.

No matter what physical limitations I had, I could perceive. I could observe. Back in the day, I was very well known for being able to read my opponents and predict their actions. I used that skill set as my guide. Perception. Observation. This I could do. How I translated what I was perceiving, breaking them down into single, understandable chunks became what I now call the "Five Pillars".

What else could I do?

I could *move*.

I couldn't move as fast as I used to, but I could move. I had no debilitating injuries, no artificial hips, knees or shoulders. I wasn't lame. I could move. I didn't have many of the youthful attributes of 30 years ago so I decided to re-hardwire the system. The first thing I did was take assessment of not what I couldn't do anymore, but of what I could do. The number of kicks and punches were limited. The head high kicks were out. My lateral kicks (round kick, hook kick and side kick) were pretty much useless. My hips were tighter than drumheads. Okay, front kick, straight punch, back fist were going to be my bread and butter moves.

Physically, I made other trades. I traded:

- Speed for fluidity
- Strength for structure
- Explosive take off for initial move (moving the attack and entry footwork at the same time)
- Raw speed for timing
- Flexibility for precision

In fact, everything was precision. That handled the body. That gave me physical guidelines. There is one common denominator to the Five Pillars. The Five Pillars all boil down to perception so we'll take them up first.

The Five Pillars are subdivisions of the overall quality of perception.

The Five Pillars to the Super Dan Method of Free-fighting are:

- Monitoring (to watch something, especially for a purpose)

- Timing (a decision of "when")

- Positioning (how and where you stand in relation to your opponent)

- Distancing (the amount of measurable space between two objects, people, etc.)

- "Zanshin" (remaining mind)

Physical attributes such as speed, quickness, strength, flexibility, coordination and the like take a back seat to these five. These five are interdependent and actually are circular, so to speak.

Your Monitoring might be first rate, but if you are out of position, your offense or defense will not be effective. Your Positioning might be first rate, but if your Monitoring is off or your timing is shaky, you will still be ineffective. You might have spot on Timing, but if your Monitoring is off or if you are out of position, that timing will be wasted on getting into position instead of immediately launching an attack or mounting a defense. If your Distancing is off, you will either be too close to execute an effective defense or too far away to launch an effective offense. If you do not have Zanshin, you could get hit during attention lapses. These five work together.

These are the key elements upon which everything else rests. You can have all of the most wonderful attributes in the world, but if you don't put these five elements to use, your free-fighting will not be as effective as it can be.

How did I come up with these exact Five Pillars? They have been important and I have stated the importance of them throughout all my books on karate but they really rose to the surface when I began my latest research project – "senior free-fighting" – me free-fighting at age 64. Back in the day, I worked very hard to make the best use of my talent. I was able to do all of the smooth moves of the day; double and triple kicks, fighting with my hands down and not get hit, explosive footwork, and so forth. Well, that was 30-40 years ago and the body does age. When I decided to undertake the project to shift from a "young Super Dan" style of free-fighting to a "present time Super Dan" style of free-fighting, one which uses a 64 year old body executing effective free-fighting, this meant acknowledging that all the talent and physical based attributes of yesteryear were honestly of yesteryear and now it was time to act my age. One thing in my favor is, I know is that principles are principles no matter how old one is. They remain constant. These were the five principles I settled on and have been basing my free-fighting on them.

Attributes vs. Principles…

Youthful attributes fade. Sorry to say but they do. Bill "Superfoot" Wallace doesn't kick as fast as he used to. At the time of this writing he's 70 years old so he's not really expected to. I am now 64. My body doesn't move like it did at 24 or 34. That's to be expected. Youthful attributes such as speed, flexibility, reaction time and so forth deteriorate with the gradual wearing out of the body. Gradual wearing out of the body = age. There's no escaping it. One can deter the effects by good diet, exercise, a positive attitude and so on but the body does wear out.

24 year old kicking ability

I had my first experience with body parts wearing out in 1997. I had trouble reading certain size print. I began having to hold a book an exact length from me in order to make the letters clearly stand out. I finally got my eyes checked and found out that I had to wear reading glasses. This pissed me off to no end. My vision was going and I hadn't "earned" it. I could explain everything else. I wasn't as limber as I used to be because I stopped stretching. My cardio was shot because I didn't train hard. But my eyes? I have never had any kind of eye injury! What the hell was up with this? They were just plain wearing out.

I remember reading in the book, The Karate Masters by Jose Fraguas, a number of interviews with seasoned karate masters, all past 50 years of age. One recurring line among all of them was that you couldn't train in your 50s the same way as you trained in your 20s. The body changes. The body wears out. The youthful attributes fade.

An interesting point I want to make at this time in my life is that the better honed your physical attributes are, the sloppier you can be with the principles. A great example is timing. The faster you can move, the larger window you have with your timing. Your speed can make up for you executing just a hair late. Flexibility and agility can cover up positioning errors. And so on. But once the natural talent and physicality begin to fade, the more you need to rely on principles as far as the Super Dan Method of Free-fighting goes. Principles do not wear out. This is where the Five Pillars come in. I have nothing against physical attributes. I relied on them for years and even when I used the principles, the youthful attributes allowed me to make use of them. But when the attributes diminished, the principles kept me in the running.

The key principles are based on perception, so let's get into them.

Monitoring – The First Pillar

Monitoring. The definition of the word monitor is:

- To watch something, especially for a purpose.

I initially teach this as a manner to see what attack is coming at you, so that you can handle it effectively. It is far more than that, but I'll take that aspect up first.

I teach two points of monitoring when spotting attacks VISUALLY. For specifically recognizing what attacks are coming, I teach watching the hands. Watching the hands is for actually blocking or parrying attacks thrown at you. For purposes of using defensive footwork, I teach watching the shoulders. These two come under the headings of *attack monitoring* and *body movement monitoring*.

Attack Monitoring...

I went over a lot on the subject of monitoring in my first book. Monitoring is my way of describing my method of attack recognition. What I have my students do is to watch the attacking agents, the hands. I feel this is the most exact part of your opponent's body to watch. There are many schools of thought concerning this. Some watch the eyes, some watch the chest, some watch the shoulders. I feel watching the hands is the best. Why do I watch the hands? I like to watch the actual attack itself. We learn this as children in a different arena. What are you told to do before crossing the street? To look both ways. Why? So you don't get hit by a car. So what is the big deal about that? You'll get hurt – pain is involved! Notice that you aren't told to listen to see if you hear traffic coming or use your sense of smell to locate cars on the road. You are told to "look both ways. It is the same with watching the hands.

I look at the hands.

What about spotting kicks coming at you if you are looking at the hands? There is a simple adjustment you can make to handle that. If you tilt your head slightly forward, your range of vision will cover from the hands to the thighs. Peripheral vision from side to side is 180-210 degrees. Top to bottom is 135 degrees, hence the tilt. You will catch any motion of your opponent's thighs in the periphery of your vision. It works like a charm. This will cover spotting any telegraph of any kick or punch your opponent will throw. Note: a telegraph is a hint or tell-tale action that shows what you are going to do prior to delivery. A non-martial arts example of this is a pitcher winding up before he throws a pitch. What's he going to do with the ball with a huge wind up like that? He's going to throw it over the plate. You will see telegraphs in boxing when a fighter draws his lead hand back to fire a hook punch. It is a seen preparatory move for the technique. This is what you are watching for. Now that you are watching for a telegraph of your opponent's motion, let's lay out how you will tell what he is going to throw at you.

A key mistake that many people make is that they will watch for *recognition of commitment* rather than *recognition of telegraph*. They'll wait that split second to see if it is a real attack coming at them. That's how you get hit. You will start your defense too late. I'll cover "too late" in the next section on timing but for right now, watch for the slightest motion of your partner's/opponent's hands. That is the telegraph of what he is going to do.

Monitoring her hands while titling my head to catch her thighs in the periphery of my vision.

My range of vision goes from her hands down to her thighs.

If you watch the hands without tilting your head, you'll run into the liability of not seeing a kick coming at you.

If you watch the hands while tilting your head, you'll be able to catch both the punch and kick.

Let's get technical. There are three parts to the cycle of action of an attack:

1. Point of origin (where they start the attack from, a fighting guard, from the hip, etc.),

2. Travel route (straight line, curved, downward, upward, etc.) and

3. Point of destination (the target).

When you watch the hands, you have your eyes on point 1, the origin point. When they move, you see it immediately. Okay, that is step one. Step two is how can you tell what is coming at you?

When you are monitoring your opponent's hands and thighs, you aren't watching for recognition of what technique is coming. That is too late. What you are looking for is a *telegraph* of the technique. You are looking for the beginning of the technique. You are looking at the first four inches of movement which tells you what is coming. This is crucial. If you are looking to recognize what the move ends up being, you will find out by being hit with it. Spotting the telegraphing action of the technique is the key.

How I do it is this: I watch his hands in conjunction with what I call the Positional Center Line. If you use both sides of your opponent's body as outer boundaries and mentally draw a line down the middle of those boundaries, you have the Positional Center Line. It will not matter if your opponent is facing forwards, angled, or sideways to you. He will have a Positional Center Line. How his hands and feet move in relation to that line gives you the information you need to read his attacks.

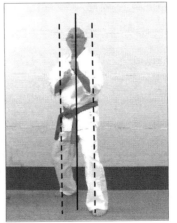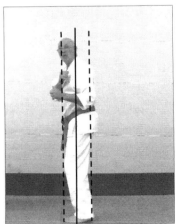

The parameters are set by the outside edges of the body. The Positional Center Line is down the exact middle of those parameters.

When your partner is facing forward, their right and left legs are on either side of the Positional Center Line.

When your partner is facing sideways, their right and left legs are both on the Positional Center Line.

Let's first take up attack recognition regarding the hands. Simply speaking, if his hand crosses the center line he is set up to throw a back fist sort of strike. If his hand moves away from the center line, his strike will come at you in a curve. If it just goes at you from its position, it's coming straight at you.

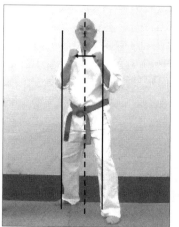 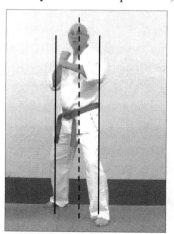 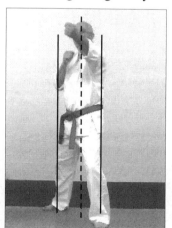 

The hand crossing over the Positional Center Line telegraphs some sort of backhand strike. Your opponent might even pose his fighting guard in a way that telegraphs his intention to strike with a back fist (last photo). A number of fighters do this.

A punch moving away from the Positional Center Line will curve back in to complete the strike.

Note that the straight punch neither crosses over or moves away from the Positional Center Line.

This holds the same for kicks as well. Tilting your head forward so that you see the thighs in the periphery of your vision, you will see the thighs move upwards to position for a kick. You will easily see the foot at the end of the leg. The way the foot is positioned for a particular kick will tell you which kick your opponent is set up for. The foot moving away from the center line will either be a round or hook kick, depending on which side it goes. If the body is sideways and the foot is exactly on the center line, it'll usually be a side kick. If the body is forwards and the foot neither crosses nor moves away from the center line, it'll be a front kick. Once you get the hang of training your observation, it will come easy to you.

The fron.t kick, much like the straight punch, does not move away from the Positional Center Line in its execution

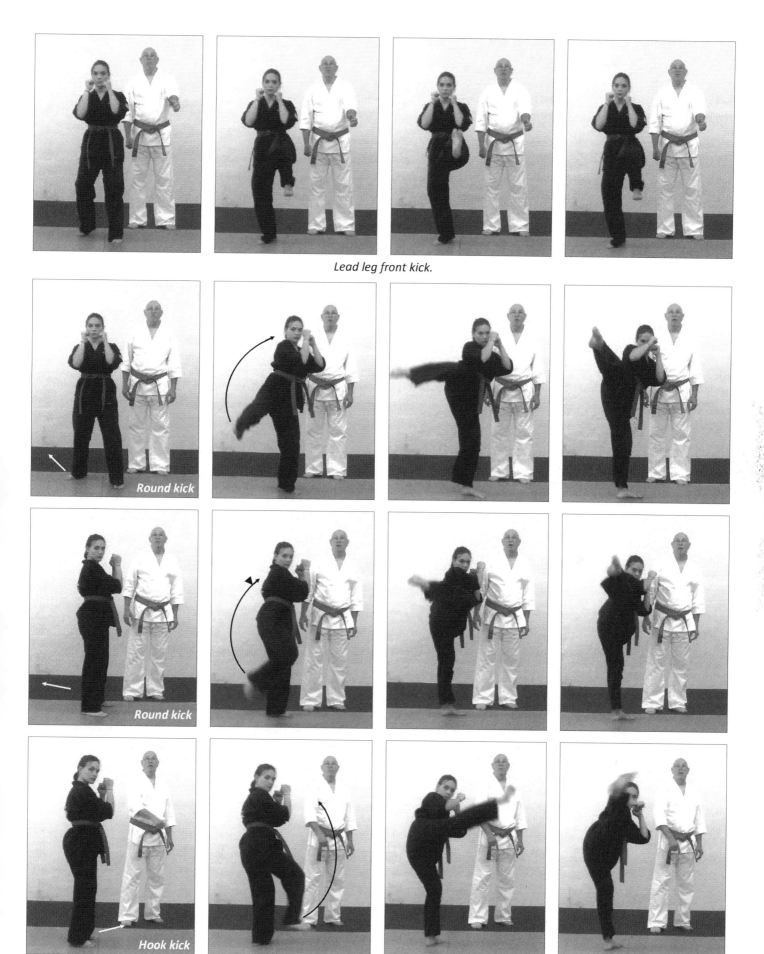

Lead leg front kick.

Round kick

Round kick

Hook kick

The round and hook kicks share the same characteristic of initially moving away from the Positional Center Line to fire.

The side kick, much like the front kick, does not move away from the Positional Center Line at the beginning of its execution.

I will tell you why I am so certain of these telegraphs. A fighter will set himself up to throw a technique from the easiest position to throw it from. In other words, a person will not try to make it hard for himself. Here is something I run in the seminars I teach. Test it out for yourself. Put your forward leg in a toes facing forward position. What is the easiest kick to throw from there? Front kick, round kick, side kick or hook kick? That is an easy one. Now test the same for which kick from each of these positions: toes at a 45 degree angle, foot totally sideways, toes slightly turned inwards from a sideways position (pigeon toed). You'll find that there is one kick for each position that is the easiest for that position. Go back and look at the foot positions in the last series of photos. Later, in your sparring, check it out. This will help greatly for spotting a kick telegraph.

As I said earlier in this text, there are different schools of thought regarding watching for telegraphs. The Super Dan Method uses watching the hands because it is the one sure-fire method that will tell you what attack is coming at you.

I *don't* watch the eyes because the eyes can't attack me. Pure and simple. I'll look at my opponent's eyes briefly to read how my opponent feels. Is he scared, angry, confident, crazy? The eyes will tell me that, but not much else. Your opponent might look at his intended target before he hits and then again he might look one place and hit another. For fighting, for me, the eyes are too unreliable.

I *don't* watch the chest. Watching the chest comes from boxing, a shirts-off sport. If the shirt is off you can see the muscles flex prior to a strike if your opponent is developed enough for the flex to be seen. Most people wear shirts, so I don't find it very reliable. The same with karate people. They wear jackets. It's hard to see the muscles flex through the jacket.

I *don't* watch the shoulders (for blocking) because although the shoulders will telegraph movement or motion, they won't telegraph the actual attack. Watching the shoulders isn't quite precise enough for me to rely on. I will watch the shoulders, however, if I'm going to use defensive angling. More on that later.

I watch the attacking agents. This has been the most effective method of attack recognition I have experienced and it has been effective for everyone I have taught it to. Make sure that if you adopt it, that you see the hands in the top range of your vision so that you can see the thigh in to lower range. This way you can spot all of your opponent's attacks, the real ones and the fakes. Speaking of fakes, after using this method for a while, you'll be able to spot when they try to fake with ease.

Translating Monitoring Into Active Defense...

Learn how to recognize what kind of blow is coming your way is the first step. The second step is the handling portion of it. Simply stated, you can handle any attack by:

- Physically stopping it (blocking)

- Diverting its path (parrying)

- Shielding the target (covering) or

- Removing the target (evasion).

A block/stop action is generally used against an attack that comes at you in a curved path, such as the hook punch, round or hook kick, ridge hand strike, etc. A parry/diversion works for attacks which come at you in a straight line, such as straight punch, front kick, backfist, etc. A shield/cover can work against pretty much any attack.

In the Super Dan Method, both hands are used for defense. A system I devised to handle the confusion of which hand is used for what purpose is called "same-siding". This is actually a common action in boxing. Your left hand handles what is coming to your left side and your right hand takes care of what is coming to your right side. You mirror your partner. His right hand is facing your left hand. Anything he does with his right hand you take care of with your left hand. He does a straight punch with his right hand. You parry it with your left hand. He does a front kick with his right leg. You parry it with your left hand. It is that simple.

With kicking, it depends on what side of your body the kick is coming at you. A right leg round kick will come at your left side so you handle it with your left arm. A right leg hook kick, however, will come at the right side of your body so you handle it with your right arm.

Same-siding against straight punch (above) and front kick (below).

37

Same-siding against round kick (above) and hook kick (bottom left). Side kick is the exception to the rule as it comes straight at you and not from the left or right side of the Positional Center Line.

How do you develop same-siding as an effective defense method? Simple. You take it in baby steps. First you take any one attack. Let's use the straight punch as an example. You teach the "correct defense" for that punch. This would be the parry in the Super Dan Method. You drill that until you can see and handle a punch coming at you from either arm. When you drill it, start out slowly. You want to go at a speed where you can analytically look at and handle the punch. I cannot overstress this. In the Super Dan Method we are looking to handle and get rid of any flinch responses. Starting out slowly is the most effective way I have found to do this.

Recognition is faster than analytical thought…
Once you can do the above easily, you can proceed to move faster and faster. An interesting thing that I have found out over the years is that analysis precedes recognition. As one begins in martial arts (or any endeavor for that matter) one has to train at the basics to become familiar with them. This is especially true with working an effective defense. You have to train the parry and train the eye to see the punch coming at you so that you can actually use that parry. Speed has a lot to do with it. If the punch comes at you too fast, you will flinch, pull away, or duck to protect yourself instead of using that parry. So, you train slowly and safely to that you can develop it. As you become more and more familiar with seeing the attack, you begin to recognize it as it develops. After a while, it will naturally register in your mind what it is without you having to think or figure it out.

A good comparison is if you have twins for nephews in your family. At first, you have to figure out what sets the two boys apart. Johnny has a rounder face while Jim has funny looking ears and so on. After you are around the twins for some time, you don't have to look for the differences. You recognize them right away without having to go through the mental checklist of differences between them. Johnny is Johnny and Jim is Jim. It is the same with recognizing what your partner/opponent is going to throw at you. It may take some time to reach this ability but you will do so with enough training.

Connection…

The final note to make is the connection between perception and connection. One can perceive and still get hit. Once you perceive you still need to connect with your partner/opponent. This is an interesting point to make as the usual concept is that you're fighting against an opponent. Fighting. Opposition. Struggle. Win-lose. Battle. Someone to overcome. All of this equals resist. That which you resist you will have a hard time connecting up with.

If free-sparring, you are training with a partner. What do you do with a partner? You work with. In order to work with, you must connect with him in some form or another. There is mutual working towards a known goal. Regarding defense, the known goal is you being able to handle his attacks with the least amount of mental and physical strain possible. Once you achieve that goal, you can begin to free-fight more easily.

Connecting with your partner/opponent…

When you begin to free-fight, you still need to decide that you are going to handle the attacks he throws at you. You need to connect with your opponent. You might ask, *"When I am perceiving my opponent aren't I also connecting with him at the same time?"* That is a fair question. My answer is, *"No."* You can perceive without connecting very easily. A good example of this is driving past an auto accident. The cars are off to the side of the road busted up. The police are there investigating and taking down information. You are in a line of cars moving on by and observing what is going on. You are perceiving but not connecting. There is no involvement on your part. I've seen people spar like that. Their defenses are highly honed, camouflaged flinches. There is no participation in actually doing something about their opponent's attacks. It's move or cover up or slap at the kick or some such.

In order to actually do something about you're your opponent's strikes, you need to connect with your opponent. You need to actively participate. This is both a mental process and a physical one. Attack Monitoring helps you with both. You can see the attack coming at you. That's a big one. If you see it coming, you can do something about it. Positioning (which we will come to much more in depth later in the text) is also key. In the beginning of sparring training, I will have my students put their hands where they can see them as well as their partner's hands. This also creates a connection. From there, it is easier to block and parry your opponent's attacks.

How do you create a connection with your partner? Well, the partner sets the stage by:

1. Not being dangerous and

2. Not being tricky.

Let's take point number 1. Martial arts moves are inherently dangerous. A punch or kick coming at you, even in the best of circumstances, represents danger. A person will naturally react to danger. I've found the most common reaction to danger is moving away from it. In other words, disconnecting from that danger. That is natural. In order to connect with your partner, your partner then needs to not be dangerous. That is simple logic. How does he accomplish this? By moving slowly and smoothly enough so that you can develop your responses to him without flinching. You might ask, *"What the hell kind of fighting is that?"* Well, it isn't. Not yet. This is development.

Point number 2 is that, while your partner is implementing point number 1, he isn't allowed to sucker you. This is very important. This could give you the false impression that you will never get skilled enough to free-fight in the long run. My opinion is that is a totally false impression. Anyone can develop to become a skilled free-fighter – anyone! It is all in the preparatory training. Learning how to connect with your partner is a huge part of that development.

How did I figure this out? By accident. Remember in the beginning I said I was afraid of getting hit? I became a defensive fighter. Because of that fear, I really watched my sparring partners and opponents. Rather than concentrate on what I was going to do to them, I concentrated on what I was going to keep them from doing to me. I was not going to get hit – not if I could help it. A friend of mine, Kara Mack, loves to tell the story of how she and I were sitting together at a karate match and I was telling her what each fighter was going to do before they did it. I developed the skills of Monitoring to keep myself from getting hit. What I didn't know for many, many years was in doing so, I also connected with my opponent. This concept of connection makes sense of one question I've had in the back of my mind for years: *"Why can I teach monitoring to students and they still get hit?"* They haven't connected. Why haven't they connected? Probably because I never brought the subject up. That's what I was doing, but never articulated it. Now I have. Develop connecting first with your sparring partner. This will help you connect with an opponent later down the road.

By the way, connecting with the opposition is hardly new. Muhammad Ali was a pro at this. His best example of this, in my opinion, was his fight with George Foreman. He had a plan of moving during the fight, fighting George like the Ali of former years. Foreman, however, was ready for that and was cutting off the ring. Instead of following Ali like a dog on a leash, when Ali moved sideways, George did too. Ali saw that he would tire out in very short order, so he changed his tactics and backed up to the ropes. This was a suicidal move in everybody's eyes…except Ali's. Big George accepted the invitation and came in and began pounding on Ali. Ali, instead of getting ready for his destruction, was *connected.* He avoided George's big punches and ended up knocking him out in the 8th round.

There is a beginning drill that I use to establish connection, which I call "token blocking". Your partner throws a series of punches or kicks at you smoothly and without power. You reach out and touch each attack. You are not actually blocking the attack. You are intercepting and connecting with it. It is done "pitty-pat" much like a children's game, but the yields arc great. Connection with your partner begins here.

In "token blocking" you connect with your partner rather than actually defend. This raises your ability to perceive your partner without flinching. The importance of this drill done with both punches and kicks cannot be emphasized enough.

The "token blocking" drill can be done with alternating kicks or multiple kicks with the same leg.

Body Motion Monitoring…

When I teach evasion, I use what I call *body motion monitoring*. Rather than looking to spot the telegraph of the actual attack, body motion monitoring is used to spot the telegraph of movement. For this, I watch the shoulders of my partner. No matter how a person moves at you, their shoulders will move before or as their body launches. More often than not, a person will use some tell-tale motion of their shoulders that telegraphs the beginning of their motion. The shoulders might drop or lean forward or turn or raise. The shoulders, if you watch them, will move before the body will launch.

This is key for evasion. You move right when you spot the tell-tale motion of your partner's shoulders. That's when you go. A huge mistake to make is to wait until you recognize the commitment of your partner. That is way too late, especially if your partner has a quick take off.

Evasion defense, stepping…

You can evade by stepping (angle steps, side steps, retreating, etc.) or moving a portion of your body out of the path of the attack (such as in bobbing and weaving).

In order to use a stepping defense you need distance between you and your partner/opponent. If you are going to move ,you need room within which to move.

You can use a step defense against your partner/opponent having to step in at you. If he is close enough to reach out and hit you, you are too close to use a stepping defense. A big problem I have had with using evasion as a defense is that it is often a camouflaged flinch reaction. When I teach evasion I use a different emphasis. Evasion is used for repositioning yourself for a better advantage, to realign yourself to your advantage. This takes the flinch out of it and keeps you in a "cause" state of mind. More on that later.

The extension of her rear leg front kick is the closest to her that I want to stand. At this distance is where I watch her shoulders.

In order to hit me she has to take a large move. This gives me time to use a footwork evasion defense.

Slight turn

Example one: I move when I see a slight turn of her shoulders.

Example two: Her shoulders drop slightly as she begins her step (note the bending of her knees in photo 2).

Example three: Her shoulders move forward as she begins her kick.

43

Your footwork evasion needs to take into account that you are moving the entire body when you evade. In doing so, you want to keep your hands up and land in a position where you can immediately launch a counter attack. I'll come back to this later in this manual when I get into the different tactics and strategies you can employ when you free-fight. This section is for learning how to free-spar.

Evasion defense, body action…

When your partner/opponent is too close for you to safely use a stepping defense you can still shift your body so that the attack does not land on the target. This is where ducking, bobbing and weaving, slipping, repositioning the target, all come into play. I go back to watching the hands when I do this. An important point to make is since you are so close to your partner or opponent, it is wise to immediately counter-attack after your first defense. Attempting to make your opponent miss over and over again takes a high degree of skill as well as some luck. It is better to start firing back right away.

Here is a datum that I have found to be true and will help you in learning defensive skills: your opponent is striking at you, usually at a specific target. If he is striking at you, he isn't striking to miss. Now here is an important point regarding targets. Targets are not that big. How big is your head? Your stomach? Your ribs? Your groin? Not all that large. This means you do not need to move the target very far in order to make your opponent miss it. A flinch reaction (shown below) will cause you to remove the target too much and actually take you out of position to counter attack. If you move out of the way of an attack, but reduce or eliminate the possibility of countering, you and your opponent are still at square one. Neither of you have an advantage.

This is a portion of a bulletin I hand out to my students:

"When I am stepping defensively to make my opponent miss yet, I am setting myself up for an immediate counter attack, I invoke *the Patriot Act*. If you have seen the Mel Gibson movie *The Patriot*, there is a scene early on in the movie where he and his two youngest sons are going to rescue his oldest son from the English army. He asks his kids if they remember what he taught them when hunting. He says, *'Aim small, miss small'*.

"My twist on that is this – the part of your opponent's body that is going to hit you is really rather small. His fist, his foot, his elbow, they are really small in proportion to his entire body. The target he is striking at is also rather small. Your head, your belly, your groin, they all cover a relatively small portion of your overall body. Therefore his *'aim is small'*. All you need to do is step enough to make him miss. A small step will make him *'miss small'*. This is the *Patriot Act*. You step small in order to make him miss small. When he misses small and you retain your alignment to him, you will be in position to fire of a counter attack right away."

This holds true for using body evasion defense as well.

How do I teach this? Not in the old-fashioned karate way. The usual karate way is to pull your blow and not strike your partner. That is a nice way of teaching you how to miss your target and your partner how to get hit by a real strike. I go about it differently. I will have my partner use a palm push (not an impact, but a nudge) to my forehead. If I miss my defense, I get reminded right away but without the pain or injury. This works beautifully.

The karate pose.

Using a gentle push instead of an impact is a safe way to learn how to get out of the way of a strike.

Aim small, miss small.

There are two more subdivisions of Monitoring that I need to go over before I conclude this section. They are: Proprioception and External Monitoring.

Proprioception…

Definition:

- The unconscious perception of movement and spatial orientation arising from stimuli within the body itself. In humans, these stimuli are detected by nerves within the body itself, as well as by the semicircular canals of the inner ear.

Boy, that's a mouthful. Let's make it easier and use a layman's definition given to me by a student of mine who is a professor of physiology and anatomy (Thanks to Susan Spencer):

- Knowing the position of the parts of your body without having to look at them

This is a lot easier to think with than the technical definition. Proprioception deals with knowing what position you are in at any given time. This comes with very thorough drilling on your basics. Diligent training in kata thoroughly develops this type of monitoring.

When you first begin learning karate, it can be like learning how to eat with chopsticks…with your left hand. Manipulating chopsticks is not an unnatural action for the hand to do, but it is certainly an untrained action for the hand. This means that you practice over and over and over in order to physically manipulate the chopsticks to a point where you do not have to think about how to use them. It is the same with karate movements. They are not unnatural actions for your body, but they are certainly untrained actions. You do them repetitively until they are second nature.

Then you start all over again with your sparring training. It's a case of "left handed chopsticks" when working with a partner, but you keep at it until that becomes second nature as well. You end up being positioned naturally and now don't have to think of how your body is positioned. You know. A statement such as "I didn't know that my lead hand was down." is indicative of not having trained the basics well enough. This is not an accusative statement because I've uttered that statement far too often myself. It just means it's time to go back to the dojo and drill some more until you know where every part of your body is at any given time. This is not a short term process but has high value in the end run.

External monitoring…

External Monitoring deals with expansion of your awareness to beyond your opponent. I developed this early on in the tournament game to where I knew which judge called a point and which didn't. Here is a good story from my memoirs, *Super Dan – A Martial Arts Memoir*, that exemplifies external monitoring.

"I mentioned about mental presence in the ring. This was also a strong point of mine. I knew everything that was going on at all times when I was fighting. The 1975 Western States Karate Championships was a prime example of what I mean. I was fighting Tom Levak for the Grand Championship. This was when my cocky arrogance was at a peak and the spectators had just about enough of me. They were waiting for me to lose. They didn't care to who just so long as I lost. I'm in the match with Tom and we are tied. We were in overtime. I threw a kick and he caught it. He fired off a kick to my groin. I guarded it with my fist. He then fired off two punches and I covered up with my arm. Four flags were in the air. The crowd went crazy! The mouth had been beaten! Tom was leaping around the ring in joy. In the words of comedian Jeff Foxworthy, *"It was pandelerium!"* I was calm. No one had caught what I had seen.

"Back then the scoring point had to be a specific action confirmed by three out of the five judges. When Tom was hitting at me there was a delay between the first two judges calling a point and the second two judges calling for a point. Two had called the kick and two had called the punch. Like a lawyer in a courtroom asking a question he already knows the answer to, I asked the chief referee for confirmation. Two judges called the kick. Two judges called the punch. The referee was Randy Zapp, a black belt from the Oregon Karate Association, who was my junior. I looked at him with the evil eye and he got the silent message: *"Don't you dare even think of calling the point!"* He called *"No confirmation."* The crowd erupted into a cascade of boos and catcalls. Knowing I was now living on borrowed time, I charged across the ring and hit Tom squarely in the chest with the winning punch. More boos. Most fighters would have seen the four flags go up and rolled with the inevitable. Not me."

External monitoring is having enough attention to spare so that you can be aware of everything that is around you while engaging with a sparring partner or free-fighting opponent. This also takes time to develop and is dependent on how calm and confident you are in your own abilities.

Attention units...

Monitoring (attack recognition and body movement recognition), proprioception/ monitoring internal (being able to "see" by recognition of position, timing, and so forth), monitoring external (attention on what is going on external to you), all deal with *attention units*.

I figure everybody has (for the sake of simplicity) 100 attention units. When you are focused on a subject or endeavor, you have nearly all or all 100 units on that one thing. The more dispersed you are, the less number of attention units are focused. This is a simple way to think about handling attention. Developing good, solid basics takes attention units off of yourself and allows you to put them on someone else. Worry takes your attention units and puts them on yourself. If you have good basics, that factor is eliminated. Skill in application of and understanding the Five Pillars allows you to take the attention units off of yourself and put them on your partner/opponent. The first step is developing good, solid basics followed by learning how to Monitor.

This illustrates the concept of taking your attention units and placing them on your opponent.

Timing – The Second Pillar

Everyone has a good sense of timing, but very few people have a workable definition of the term. My own working definition of timing is:

- Timing is a decision of "when".

When what? When anything. As I said, everyone has a good sense of timing in daily life. You lift a fork to your mouth, your mouth opens just at the right time to take a bite. Timing. You approach a door. Your feet slow down and halt so that you don't run into it while you extend your hand to open it. Timing. You decide to pass another car on the freeway. You look to see if there are other cars nearby, you accelerate to pass the car, and you finish by pulling ahead of the car far enough so that you don't hit it. Timing.

All of these examples include a decision of when. Even if certain timing usages are now reflexive, they began with a decision of when. Okay, let's now get into free-fighting use of timing – when to attack. I find the best time to attack my opponent is on a moment of change, when he changes in any way, shape, or form.

The concept of Attention Units is crucial also in the application of timing. I consider that everyone has 100 measurable units of attention. If my opponent has all 100 of his attention units zeroed in on me, he is going to spot when I am going to come forward to attack. His eyes are on me with no distractions present. There is no way I am going to sneak anything past him.

Now, if he steps, shifts his weight, changes his hand position, anything, he will use some of his attention units to do that. That is "x" amount of attention units less on me. This is when I launch an attack. You might say, *"Well, he isn't thinking 'Now I'm going to move my hand down a quarter of an inch. Okay, now I've done that. I'm done.'"* The fascinating thing is this works on even a subconscious level. If a person moves from a totally still position, some of his attention units will be in play and that is that amount of attention units that will be off of you, even if only for a split moment. You might ask *"What if he isn't stock still? What if he's moving?"* My answer is that he won't have all 100 of his attention units on you in the first place. You still hit him on the change.

She has all of her attention units on me (photo 1). She begins to step back with her lead foot siphoning off attention units to her step. This is when I take off with my attack (photo 2). I arrive with my attack before she can fully respond (photo 3).

When your opponent shifts a portion of his attention units this opens up a door, a window of opportunity to go forward to attack him. Following are some examples of "the door opening".

In the above two sequences the moment I begin my step, the door opens for her to punch me.

This is something you can work with to good effect. I have found this concept to be uniformly workable when training students at my school and in seminars. An example of an everyday life event would be if you are studying for school and your buddies are having a party. The are loud and the stereo is turned up and the music is playing. You are trying to concentrate on your assignment and your are distracted. Attention units are being siphoned off by what is going on outside of your study area. This phenomenon happens everywhere. Have you ever avoided getting into a car accident? I have. Look back at a time when this happened and see if you can spot where your attention was at the time. You might have been singing to the radio. You might have had a problem on your mind. Maybe you were looking forward to your next date with your girlfriend. You were robbed of some attention units by something. This is such an every day phenomenon that it tends to get overlooked. Don't overlook this when you free-fight. Use it to your advantage.

Which changes do you hit him on? There are many changes you can spot but some of the most obvious ones are:

- The moment he steps forward
- The moment he steps back
- The moment he steps to the side
- The moment he shifts his weight forward or back
- The moment he raises his lead hand (shown below)
- The moment he lowers his lead hand (shown below)
- The moment he changes moving from one side to the other
- The moment he raises up from his stance
- The moment he lowers himself deeper in his stance
- The moment he shifts from a side facing position to a front facing position (and vice versa)

The list can go on and on and is limited only by your imagination and observation. I tend to watch my opponent's hands (detailed previously in the section on Attack Monitoring) or his shoulders to catch changes in my opponent (detailed in section on Body Motion Monitoring).

Timing trigger - your opponent rests back in his stance.

Timing trigger - your opponent begins to step back.

Timing trigger - your opponent begins to kick.

You'll note that all of the example timing triggers have one thing in common. Change. Change in position as he begins his action. When there is change, there are divided attention units. There is not necessarily divided attention. Your opponent might feel all of his attention is still on you and it will be on a conscious level. On a subconscious level, however, attention units will be siphoned off. If you are spot on with your timing, your opponent might feel you are too fast for him or have some other reason for getting hit by you. One of my biggest weapons was my judgement of timing. My timing was very good because I understood what it was. Now you do as well. It takes training to set your body into motion right at the beginning of your opponent's move, but it can be trained.

Okay, what if you do the drills but feel your timing is still off? That comes next.

Errors in timing...

Now that you have a definition of timing, why might your timing be off? Simple. Since timing is a decision of when, your "when" is most likely be off, which brings me to the next point – how to correct your timing to make it as pinpoint as possible. There are three mistakes in application of timing. Two of them are obvious from the definition of the term itself:

- Too soon and

- Too late

My favorite example of the mistakes in timing is a kid arriving for dinner. Dinner is scheduled at 6 pm. If the kid arrives too soon he has to set the table for mom. If he arrives too late, he misses out on dinner, has to eat Cheerios for his dinner and ends up doing the dishes. If he arrives at 6 pm, all he has to do is wash his hands, sit down, and enjoy.

Too soon and too late are the key obvious mistakes in free-fighting. You attack when your opponent is ready for you and your chance of success will be slim. You attack too late and you have missed your opportunity. This runs true with defense as well. If you defend too soon you yank yourself out of position and if you defend too late, well, you just got hit. Too soon and too late. These are the obvious mistakes in timing. How do you avoid these mistakes? By keeping a watchful eye on your opponent and drilling timing.

Error in timing 1. Too soon - she hadn't changed anything so she was ready for me.

Error in timing 2. Too late - she was done changing so she was ready for me.

Now you know a working definition of timing. You also now the two key errors in timing. There is one more factor you need to be aware of if you are having any timing difficulties. Read on.

The hidden beast...

There is a third mistake in timing that nearly everyone totally misses – Preparation, lack of. Your spotting can be excellent. Your tactics can be optimum. Your ability to see the minutest changes in your opponent can be razor sharp. However, if you aren't prepared to move, they will be all for naught. Here is an example I use in every seminar I teach on timing. I will have the students execute a slide forward backfist strike when they see their partner execute a change. After three or four changes, I will ask if anyone is still having trouble with their timing. I will always get someone who is still not getting it. I will have that student do the drill in front of everyone and will ask the group to watch closely and then tell me what the very first move that student makes is. The student will do the drill for four or five repetitions. Then I ask the group what his first motion was. They always get it wrong. Always! I then tell them what I see.

More often than not the student is bending his knees first, then launching his backfist strike. In other words, his timing was spot on but he was wasting that precious split instant in time by *getting ready to move* instead of moving. He wasn't ready to move and that is the hidden factor in timing – Preparation. If you aren't prepared to go, you will first prepare to go and then go. The only problem is that you have just spent your "when" by getting ready instead of just going.

Note that in this example I drop my knees just as she drops her lead hand. My timing is spot on but it is wasted by using it to prepare to move instead of already being prepared. By the time I arrive she is ready to handle my attack.

So, here is something to look at. Are you prepared to move without hesitation? Are your knees sufficiently bent to step immediately? Are your hands in position to attack or defend without needing to reposition them in order to do so? Watch a video of you sparring and see for yourself to get your answers. Now that you have this data to work with, your timing should be easy to correct or even make better.

Caution: Here is one added thing to watch out for. You can be slightly off in your timing if you are naturally quick. This can become a camouflaged hole in your timing. I define quickness as "suddenness of movement". If you can move suddenly, you can be a hair late in your timing and your quickness can make up for it. Your "when point", the exact moment you decide to move has broader parameters than if you aren't so quick. If you aren't quick, your timing has to really be spot on. And for your timing to be spot on , you need to be prepared to move which brings us to the next pillar, Positioning.

Positioning – The Third Pillar

Positioning is how and where you stand in relation to your opponent. For me, correct positioning is:

- your being positioned so that you are ready to attack or defend.

I look at Positioning in several ways. First is offensive capability. Are you ready to launch whatever attack you want from the position you are in? If you like the back fist and side kick as your principal weapons of offense, can you launch them from right where you are without further preparation? If you are, then you are in position. If you have to do something in order to launch them, then you are out of position. It is the same with forward attacks.

As an example, one of the best examples of being in position was point fighting champion Bill Wallace. (below). Wallace was known for having only three kicks in his arsenal; the side kick, round kick, and hook kick, all off of his lead side. That was all. Everybody was amazed at his speed. His kicks were clocked at 60 miles per hour. Yes, he was fast, but even more important was that his positioning was superb. He was always ready to fire any one of those kicks. You never found him in any other position than facing sideways. It was the same with all-time great, Joe Lewis (bottom right photo, left side)

Other stellar fighters who always maintained position were Frank Smith, Tonny Tulleners and Chuck Norris. Japanese style fighters were known for paring their attacks down to front kick and straight punch. Smith's body was always forward and his limbs were always set to fire straight punch and front kick. His fists were pointed at his opponent and both of his legs were in exact position so that he could kick with either leg without hesitation. I found it was the same with Gosoku-ryu practitioner Tonny Tulleners. Chuck Norris (above right photo) often positioned himself in the same way. None of these players were out of position…ever! This is offensive positioning at its finest.

The second way I look at positioning is defensive positioning. Are you set up so that you won't get hit? Are your hands down? Are your legs not ready to move? If you get hit often, then there is something about your defensive positioning that is faulty. Two examples of excellent defensive positioning were karate fighters Jeff Smith and Joe Lewis. Both players had great defenses and both were very different. Jeff carried his hands high so as to ward off kicks and punches. Joe, on the other hand, used his quick retreat to get out of the range of an opponent's attack. He was always set to move. Two very different approaches to defense, but they both had one thing in common – their position was set up so that they could execute their defense without a moment's hesitation, with no delay.

There are three basic positions I teach in the Super Dan Method and each has their purposes, advantages and disadvantages. The first is a hybrid boxing/Thai kickboxing stand up position. The body is front-facing with the feet being a shoulder width apart. Your hands are up roughly cheek height with your forearms vertical and aligned with your shoulders. This position is a good one for luring your opponent's strikes into your defense. It is also good for any kind of straight forward offense of your own. It is not well set up to deliver lateral attacks though.

The second position is a hybrid side facing position in which you use your arms and stance to cover and hide your opponent's major target areas. In it I use my arms and elbows to cover my head, side of body and groin area. The disadvantage of this position is that it is a good one for American point karate competition but leaves your legs open to an attack.

The third position is also a good one for competition and that is using my hands to obstruct the line of attack of my opponent. An example of this is at the last tournament I competed in, I spotted one of the team players from Japan warming up. I noted that a favored tactic was to lead off with the front hand to the face. In my first match I competed against one of them, I placed my lead hand forward in direct line with his lead hand creating an obstruction for his front punch. It worked like a charm.

Standard karate stance   *Super Dan preferred stance*   *Side stance*

From a forward position I am ready to deliver a straight forward attack without needless preparation.

My forward position is inefficient for delivering a back fist strike . I have to chamber my arm first (1-4).
A standard karate stance is better for this as the back fist is aimed at my opponent (5-8).

5 - *Note that my back fist is aimed at her*

Her turn before the kick is a huge telegraph or her action which makes it easy for me to defend myself (1-6). Standing sideways and shuffling up before kicking helps hide the telegraph of it (7-12).

Structure and Alignment

Two factors that play a big part in Positioning are Structure and Alignment. To me, Structure is hugely important. Your structure will enable you to strike hard and keep your balance. Watching any kind of skilled striker, you will find one thing in common and that is he will maintain his structure.

What I mean by this is that he will either keep your upper body aligned straight over his hips or keep his shoulders from straying too far from that position of over the hips. By doing this, he can keep his weight under him and create a strong base for power blows, and also keep his balance from not overextending his strikes. This is where I could get into a long dissertation on center of gravity and go off into a physics discussion but I won't. I'm not a physicist. You almost need to be a physicist to understand most of the definitions you will find. Here is the simplest definition of 'center of gravity' I could find:

- the point within something at which gravity can be considered to act

If your structure is straight up and down, gravity pulls you down. Your center of gravity is positioned in the center of your body. This position will vary slightly between men and women as well as personal body type. If you begin to bend forward, you will feel a slight inclination to topple forward. Your center of gravity has shifted forward a little bit. The more you lean forward, the further forward your center of gravity goes.

Normal structural alignment in an uninjured body is straight up and down. Note my center of gravity (above).

The moment I lean on a strike my center of gravity goes forward and I can be toppled rather easily.

My arnis teacher, Remy Presas, would work on me was a capture and off-balancing move when I would break my structure when throwing a strike (1-6). Examples of good and poor structure during a clinch (7-12)

In American point-fighting, it is an everyday occurrence to dive in at your opponent to extend the reach of your punch. This is nice and fine for garnering a scoring tag type of hit but can be disastrous if you are in a fight or self-defense situation. You lose control over your center of gravity. In doing so, you leave yourself open for your opponent's counter punch as well as a grappler catching you off-balance and then taking you to the ground. Structure is very important in the Super Dan Method of Free-fighting.

Portland, Oregon 1967   *Mid-America Diamond Nationals 1979*   *Gresham, Oregon 2017*

And yes, I have violated this rule myself...Portland, Oregon 1977

Alignment is a blood brother to Structure and is a sub-category to Positioning. Alignment, simply stated, is how you are facing your opponent in relationship to how he is facing you. If you prefer to face your opponent from a sideways position, know your options both offensively and defensively. Know exactly what you can do and even more important, what you cannot do. This way you will be effective.

Note that in the above photos, my partner and I are aligned with each other, ready to attack or defend. If she is in a position ready to go at me with her weapons firing, she is on what I can her "line of attack". If we are both on our lines of attack, we are on the Connection Line. We are connected. In terms of alignment, what I want is to be on my line of attack while she is not. I will get more into the applications of this in the section on defensive movement, but suffice it to say that you want to have your alignment such that you can attack your opponent without having to do extra preparation. In the Super Dan Method, I prefer a forward position. If I am in a forward position, I have four weapons available – two hands and two feet. I don't want to shift my position so that I end up with three or two weapons for immediate release. If I step off of my opponent's line of attack and maintain my four weapon position, I will have a superior position, even if only for a moment.

If you prefer to face your opponent from a sideways position, know your options both offensively and defensively. Know exactly what you can do and even more important, what you cannot do. This way you will be effective.

Okay, back to Positioning. You have two general options for your positioning; one offensive and one defensive. The key question regarding your positioning is *"Can you immediately execute?"* That is the question. Execute what? We are looking at offense and defense here. It doesn't matter what you choose to execute. That is up to you. Can you execute what you want to from the position you are in? If not, what adjustments do you need to make? If you're not sure, video yourself and watch that. Pretty soon the answer will become clear. As a note, in the Super Dan Method of Free-fighting it is best if you can execute both your offense and defense from one position. I use two positions, one primary and one secondary position. One last statement regarding positioning is that when you know exactly what you can and cannot do from any conceivable position, you will never be out of position. This is high level proprioception and takes lots of practice and experience to reach this level but it can be done.

In the Super Dan Method, you want to keep your opponent in your sights at all times. If I am in a position where I can execute a jab and cross, I am aligned with my opponent.

Note that I keep my alignment when I angle step. This keeps me in a position where I can both attack or defend.

Distancing – The Fourth Pillar

Distance appreciation is the next of the five pillars. Back in my competition days, I was known for being able to make my opponent miss me by a hair. My observation of distance was very acute. There are actually two component parts to distancing and they are often lumped together as one concept. As you understand the difference between the two, your understanding of distancing will expand. The first concept has to do with Range.

Range, in military terms, is:

- The maximum distance a projectile weapon has to travel to be efficient. The military definition of Range is very applicable to martial arts. Range is the effective distance of any particular weapon. A kick has a longer range than a punch. A sword has a longer range than a knife while a bullet has a longer range than the sword. Range has to do with the effectiveness of any given weapon.

That's a simple one to understand. Throwing a rock has greater range than a punch. Firing a rock from a sling shot has greater range than throwing that same rock. A bullet has greater range than a rock fired from a sling shot. And so on. One can look at body weapons in the same manner. A kick has a longer range than a punch while a punch has a longer range than an elbow strike or a kick with the knee. These are very simple truths yet not understanding them can get you attempting to throw the "wrong" technique because of inappropriate range.

A working definition of distance can be:

- The amount of measured space between any two objects

That, too, is a simple one. How far is it from point A to point B? There's the distance. The terms "distancing" and "range" are often used interchangeably, however they are two distinctly different concepts in martial arts.

When you understand the difference between these two terms, you can use distance to foil your partner's and opponent's range. Let me repeat that in a different way. I use distance to negate range. This is the game you play when you begin free-sparring. The offensive player wants to establish his range for his advantage. The defensive player wants to use superior defense (blocking or blocking and countering) and distance for his advantage.

Critical Distance Line…

Understanding the concept of Range will help you set the Distance between you and your partner/opponent when you square off to spar or free-fight. You don't want to be too close or too far away. How do you go about determining that? I use the concept of the Critical Distance Line from a defensive point of view. I will stand at a distance where my opponent can barely touch me with his rear leg front kick just enough to dirty my shirt, but not impart any meaningful impact. This is how close I will stand to my opponent. If he is any closer, I will either attack or get out of his range. If he is further away than that I will move closer to get to that distance.

Critical Distance Line - Close enough to only dirty my jacket.

Now, why do I use this exact measurement of distance, the extension of my opponent's rear leg front kick? Simple. The rear leg front kick is the most powerful long range attack that has the least amount of tell-tale motion. From this distance my opponent needs to move his entire body to get into an effective range for any of his attacks. He needs to move his entire body to get to me. This creates a bigger telegraph of his action which, in turn, makes it safer for me. Round kick, side kick, and spinning kicks are all more powerful kicks and have better range than the front kick but they have one huge drawback. They all have larger body actions. Larger body actions = more telegraphs. They are easier to spot because of the actions inherent in the kicks themselves. Does this work against me in the same fashion? Of course, but I look at personal safety first.

Note how little there is in the way of tell-tale movement in the rear leg front kick.

With the rear leg round kick, she has to turn her body quite a bit in order to deliver the kick. She can reach me with the kick but it is easily seen and therefore easy to defend against.

There is a lot of action in both the shuffle up round or side kicks and spinning back, side or hook kicks prior to the kick which is easily seen when you maintain the Critical Distance Line.

When I teach this to my students, I will use two concepts to get the idea across. The first is humorous. I will tell them that the Critical Distance Line is the closest you can get to someone and still be critical of them. Same spelling, but different definition. This usually brings about a laugh but gets the point across. You don't want to stand too close to someone while you are being critical of them. Not safe. The second example is the concept of one's personal space. The concept of one's personal space is often called your "bubble." Okay. You don't let your opponent inside your bubble. That is also an easy concept to get across.

The above is a perfect example of jockeying for range. Where I am standing is perfect for me but not so good for her. She is at full extension while I am in range for impact upon extension.

Where do we begin?

In the Super Dan Method of Free-fighting, the Critical Distance Line is a defensive line, not an offensive one. When you begin to free-spar, you will want to start at a safe distance. One of the first lines of defense is being out of the effective range of your partner's attacks. When you do this you will force your partner to use big motions to land his attacks. I feel the closest to your partner you can safely be is where he can only touch your shirt with a front kick. I do not teach point competition karate where even touching the shirt will be considered landing a telling blow. A touch to the shirt is still missing your target. This is the distance from where you begin your free-sparring from. I'll go over different distances in the section on Footwork by Range later in this text.

Zanshin – The Fifth Pillar

Zanshin is one of the very few Japanese terms that I use in my school. I haven't found anything in English that really says it. There is a terrific article called "What Is Zanshin?" in the Jiyushinkai Budo News, Issue 23, written by C. Clark (2001) that covers it well and goes over the component parts of it. In this article, it says *"Translated literally, zanshin means 'left over or remaining heart/spirit' or words of similar meaning."* I have also seen it translated as *"remaining mind."* This article lists out the component parts that make up the concept of Zanshin:

- Shisei (posture)

- Metsuke (eye control)

- Ma-ai (engagement distance)

- Kiai (focused energy)

- Ki musubi (connection)

- Kime (decisive focus)

- Riai (essence of the technique)

- Kanken (intuition/awareness)

Note that Zanshin has the first four pillars contained within it (and more), but the concept of the translation puts it at the end of the engagement, the key word being "remaining". It is so easy to be prepared and ready to go at the beginning of any engagement but often energy and awareness drops off at the end, especially if you have been successful with your attack. *"Hey! I'm done. I hit him! Time for a beer!"* Not quite. It ain't over until you're clear of your opponent and totally out of his range. The end of the engagement is where you need awareness the most. This is where grapplers can have the advantage over a striker. A striker will deliver the hit and if he's not totally ready, this is where the grappler will take him down and go to work on him.

"Remaining mind" – total continued awareness after the fact – Zanshin.

Beginning awareness - beginning mind.

68

Turning your back after scoring a technique (1-6) or concentrating solely on hitting your opponent without monitoring them (7-9) can get you hit in a real encounter - lack of Zanshin.

Here is an example of Zanshin - keeping my eye on my opponent for their counter-attack as I attack.

How to develop the Five Pillars for yourself...

Remember what I said about what can I do? I can perceive. It all begins with perception. Each of the Five Pillars rely on perception. Perception of your opponent, perception of yourself, perception of your distancing, perception of positioning, perception of timing, and so on. It's all about perception. Developing all of these might seem daunting, but there is a relatively easy way to do it.

The Five Pillars work very closely together. A great way to develop them is take any one of them and concentrate only on that one for a sparring period with a partner. Then pick another one. Then pick another one. Rotate through them several times in one class or training period. What will happen is, you will begin to focus better now that you have something to focus on. This will lay the foundation for the Five Pillars to become second nature.

Keep in mind one thing, however. These will not be overnight developments. Consistent work on these three skills will take time to fully come to fruition and become a working part of your skills.

Section Three:

Movement

Section Two - Learning How To Free-Spar

This subject called free-fighting. I've figured it out so let's get down to business. I break this book down into several sections. First and very important is learning how to spar. From there, I will go over transitioning over from free-sparing to free-fighting.

I am going to repeat myself at this point. Here are several definitions of the word "spar":

- Make the motions of boxing without landing heavy blows, as a form of training.
- (Of boxers) To make the motions of attack and defense with the arms and fists, especially as a part of training.
- To fight with an opponent in a short bout or practice session, as in boxing or the martial arts

"Sparring partner":

- (Boxing) a person who practices with a boxer during training
- Someone who helps a boxer practice, someone who a boxer spars with for training

Note the use of the words "practice", "helps", and "training". Sparring is a cooperative effort. Sparring is not fighting.

Pre-frame your student...

Quite often you will hear the term "pre-frame" in the martial arts industry. This means to educate or set up a parent for what your program is about or what you are going to do in your school. Before we get onto the subject of free-fighting itself, a bit of pre-framing is needed. All too often a student is thrown into free-fighting way too soon. My favorite phrase for this is *"throwing the Christians to the lions"* meaning they get beat up by the senior students. One thing I have found out in the 48 years I have been teaching karate and arnis is that very few people are "natural fighters". Yes, people have natural survival instincts and yes, people will fight if they get mad or scared enough, but people who were "born to fight" are few and far between. They need to be educated. They need help in getting over their fears of getting hit and yes, their fear of hitting someone else as well. Just as one needs to learn how to walk before they can run, one needs to learn how to spar before they learn how to fight.

Beginnings...

The beginning stages of development of one's free-fighting skills are the most important and have to be undertaken with care. Why is this? Because most people are not natural fighters. Subconsciously, even the mildest kicks and punches represent danger. People will be shy of getting in there and doing mock battle. They will flinch like crazy. They will speed up without knowing it. Why? This is a natural response to danger. What danger? Aren't we going slowly? The danger is on an unconscious reactive level, not a conscious analytical level. Pain is involved. Present time pain? No. Past pain. The fascinating thing is that it doesn't even have to make sense. You can throw a punch at someone's head who has never been in a fight and they will flinch. Why? They have never been hit in the head. Why should they flinch from that? They have never experienced that before. Well, everybody has had some sort of head impact of some sort or another. Maybe they ran their head into a door frame. Maybe they were playing dodge ball and got hit in the face with the ball. Who knows? The common denominator is that something unexpected whacked them in the face and it hurt. It is from that premise where I begin. (Note: there is a book that thoroughly explains this phenomenon, *Dianetics: The Modern Science of Mental Health* by L. Ron Hubbard.)

I went over this briefly in a previous section regarding connection. Learning how to spar requires that you connect with your partner so that you can learn how to respond rather than react. After reading the above, it should make better sense to you. When you learn to respond, you will be more cause over how you spar so let's get further into the next aspect of pre-framing yourself to sparring, which is Cause and Effect.

Cause and effect...

There is a phenomenon or mental effect of shifting from a point of being in command and comfortable to a point of being out of sorts or ineffective when free-sparring. The effects are very real. You are doing well or feeling good about your free-sparring and then somewhere along the line it's not going so well. This can be a sudden shift or a gradual one. This is the phenomenon of Cause and Effect. Let's go over this.

- 'Cause' means you are being in command. Whatever you are doing is going well. You feel good about it.

- 'Effect' means things aren't going so well. You are now being dominated by the efforts of others.

You want to be cause in your actions. This is easy enough to do when practicing basics or kata but harder to pull off when you are free-sparring because free-sparring often turns into free-fighting, which is a game of dominance. I have a good friend who is like that. You can't spar with him. I don't believe he knows how to spar. Every time he spars he goes into battle mode and it turns into a dominance game. With him I work on battle but nothing else. How do you remain at cause when you are free-sparring and later in free-fighting? That is the thrust of this book – learning how to remain at cause in your free-fighting. The first step is understanding the definition of the words "sparring" and "sparring partner" so that you know what you are doing and choosing the right person to work with. The second is learning about your body, learning about how to move in karate.

Confronting the tools of the trade...thoroughly drilling your basics...

In any line of endeavor, whether it is work or play, you start out being unfamiliar with it. That is simple. You never did it before so you are all thumbs with it. Me sitting here writing on a keyboard is a great example. Before my 9th grade typing class, I didn't know how to type. After a semester, I had a bit of familiarity with it. Now I write books strictly using a keyboard. Here's another example. My first driving lesson from my mom was quite the experience. I nearly hit another car and then when I overcompensated the turn to avoid it, I ran the car into a ditch. I was unfamiliar with how to handle a car. Now I can drive, listen to music while I drive, and eat a cheeseburger and carry on a conversation all at the same time. I am familiar with the handling of a car.

I tell my students when they are first starting out learning karate, it is like using "left-handed chopsticks". The movements are not unnatural movements but they are certainly untrained movements. When you first learn them, they do not feel natural. After you practice them, they feel better and better until they become a part of your movement pattern. Martial arts are no different, in this manner, than typing, driving, cooking, auto mechanics, or what have you. You go from unfamiliar and through repetition to familiar. It is a simple enough process. This is where your instructor stresses basics, lots of repetitions of basics. You become familiar with how the body moves with your different kicks and punches. After a while they will feel familiar to you. Now you're ready to begin free-sparring. Or so you think.

There is one inherent factor involved that needs to be dealt with. That is the "implied pain" factor. Kicks and punches represent danger, even if on an unconscious level. What is the natural reaction to danger? There is no one reaction that everybody has but they include panic, freezing up, flinching, backing off, and so forth. So, how do I deal with that? In a couple of ways.

The first is speed of movement. There is a speed with which everyone is comfortable and once something exceeds that speed, you go out of your comfort zone. This is where you "react". In my terminology, a reaction is an uncontrolled flinch response. Several years ago I had an experience that details it nicely. I am not a skier. My wife is an excellent skier and comes from a skiing family. I never wanted to learn how to ski ever since I saw a fellow karate player who had a knee operation resulting from a skiing injury back in the late 1960s. He had a big Frankenstein-like scar on his knee and I wanted no part of that. Well, about 4 or so years ago, I was coaxed out onto the ski slopes in a big family outing. I bought a 5 day lesson plan. I was terrible at it. It took me 3 ½ days to finally make it down the lowest grade training slope without falling down. Everything in skiing was counter-intuitive to what I do in martial arts. I finally figured out how to turn and do a plow, so I spent the fourth day drilling on those specifically. On the fifth day I was ready for the first hill, the bunny slope. From the top of it I looked down. It looked a whole lot steeper than what I thought it should look like. I pushed off and started down the hill. I started going a whole lot faster than I wanted to. I immediately went into a plow position to slow myself down. It didn't work! I was going faster and faster! My mental thought process froze. I was out of my comfort zone. Instead of trying to turn, I did the only thing I could think of – I fell down. That slowed me down for sure.

But what happened here is the important thing. I got outside of my comfort zone and panicked. I flinched. This is what will happen if you free-spar at a rate of speed/power than what is comfortable for you. Oh, by the way, I continued skiing that day and figured out how to cut my speed going down that slope. I carved out a lot of turns while going down the hill, thereby cutting my speed to a manageable level.

So, what I do right from the beginning is reduce the speed of the techniques so that the beginning student is now dealing with motion and movement rather than attacks. A slowed down kick or punch, when slowed down enough, becomes a non-threating movement. This transformation is very key to initial development and I cannot stress this enough. Familiarity with the tools begins with how to do the movements of free-fighting at a speed range, power range, and impact level which is entirely comfortable to you so that you can respond rather than react. Just like driving a car or skiing down a hill or anything. You ease yourself into it.

There are all sorts of combinations of moves which will gain you familiarity with the striking aspects of martial arts. There is another factor involved here that is of prime importance. What do you do with incoming strikes? In free-fighting, this is where the rubber meets the road. It doesn't take much effort to learn how to hit a training bag or do moves watching yourself in a mirror. There is no danger there.

When someone strikes at you, however, the game changes right away. Now there is danger of getting hurt, implied or real, and this is where the fear factor sets in. I have an intimate relationship with the fear of getting hit. I had a near full blown phobia of getting hit and hurt. My imagination ran wild with this fear. Back when I first competed, I was known for my defensive abilities. Why? Because I was unspeakably awesome? No. Because I was scared of getting hit. I was scared of getting hurt. I made it a practice to never get hit if I couldn't help it. It took me many years to find out a very important fact.

The body will allow only so much pain until it protects you by going unconscious. Think about it. The pain you feel from a strike is not the pain you feel from an exposed nerve. It is much less than that. If the impact is too great, you get minimally, a dulling of the senses, a partial unconsciousness. That being said, I don't endorse taking punishment or impact blows because of this reason but if I knew that fact, I might not have been so afraid of it.

How to handle fear of free-sparring…

So what did I do to handle this fear? I learned how to read incoming blows. I learned to see how the blows are telegraphed. I also learned how to handle them. This is Monitoring and blocking and they are surprisingly simple. First, go back to the section on the Five Pillars and re-read the section on Monitoring. Second, let's briefly review what I use for defensive techniques.

I do not use a vast number of techniques for defense. In fact, I try to keep the number of actual techniques down to a bare minimum. It's bad enough to get used to seeing incoming blows. To pile on many techniques to handle them is counter productive. I like to keep it simple. Note: I am going to show all that goes into an effective defense so this particular section will not be a brief one.

I use parries to handle straight on attacks and guards/shields to handle circular attacks. How is that for being simple? I will use defensive footwork in conjunction with my techniques...or not. It all depends on my particular strategy for that exact moment. For beginning sparring, however, I stress standing still and blocking. Defensive footwork at this stage of the game tends to be a camouflaged flinch.

I use a simple side to side parry to handle straight attacks of any kind.

When I parry or guard/shield, I always use same-siding. I take care of the arm or leg that is directly in front of my arm.

When I use a parry, there are two things I always watch out for. If I can, I always apply same-siding. This is using the arm that is directly in front of your partner's attacking limb, much like what you'd see if your were doing mirror practice. I do not do one arm parries. I call that "windshield wiping". I used to take advantage of opponents who would do that. The second thing I watch out for is what I call over-blocking. I push the incoming blow just enough to make it miss me. I'll illustrate this on the flowing pages.

When using a parry I try to push from one side of my head to the other.

 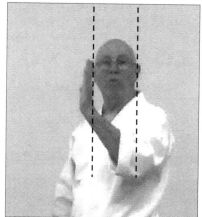

The liability of parrying with only one arm (1-2) is not being fast enough to handle two full speed attacks (3-6).

Here is an interesting point about body structure. Most straight punches actually come at you from a bit of an angle. Your arms attach at your shoulders, which are at the outside edges of your torso. In order for a punch to come in straight at you, it travels from the outside edge inward. Giving the punch a slight defensive nudge will move its trajectory past your head. This is why I like to move a punch only three inches when I make contact with it. It is already travelling at an angle so there is no point in pushing it farther. If your opponent spots that you over-parry punches, this can set you up for a fake which, leaves you open for a follow up attack.

In the above sequence, my partner has spotted that I tend to over-parry so she fakes a punch and I parry too far, missing her arm. She follows up with a second punch when my hand goes past.

I will use a forward press against a back fist strike (1-2). The sooner I can make contact with it, the better. Again, I prefer to same-side as a lead hand defense can set me up for her follow up attack (3-8).

I use a guard/shield against curved attacks, both hands and feet.

When blocking a front kick, I use the same concept of parrying or diverting the force off trajectory to its target. I was initially taught the hard downward block for the kick. This really didn't work well for me as I was pretty much using force against force and I was much too small for that. Diverting it sideways was a much better option for me. So, the big trick was how to get my arm to one side of the leg so that I could knock or pull it sideways. What worked for me is to punch my arm downward to a straight position and move it sideways from there.

I also use a "drop and pull" open handed action that I picked up from Mike Stone in a magazine article. This is more of a straight down action with your arm and then pulling the leg sideways on contact with it.

Handling a side kick poses an interesting problem. Even though it is a straight forward kick like the front kick, it doesn't come at you from a left or right hip position. It comes at you straight down the middle making it difficult to do the standard downward block as a defense against it. I find that as powerful as the side kick is, it has a fascinating weakness. Your leg in a sidekick position is incredibly weak against a straight downward force. It is easy to shove straight down hence that is the approach I take to defending against it. I use a double downward push against it to great effect. For my kids classes I nickname it "10 down".

You can use 10 down from a stationary position or add a step back for safety. Either way works very well.

Stand still

Step back

I teach a simple three-part exercise that really works in taking away the fear of strikes coming at you. It is called the Five Punch Drill. Here is the simplicity of it: you do five punches at your partner. He defends against them. Then he does five punches at you and you defend against them. You do this back and forth without a break in the motion. Here is the key to success to this drill. Your goal, as the puncher, is that your partner defends successfully against all five punches. To do this you need to punch in such a relaxed manner so that there is zero chance of your partner making a mistake. In fact, if your partner misses a block or parry, you are the one who did something wrong. Get it?

In doing this drill, do not worry about speed and power. That will come as you and your partner become more and more familiar with how to read incoming attacks and defend against them. You expand this drill to become a Five Kick drill and then a combination Five Attack drill using kicks and punches. If you do this over and over again you will become more relaxed in the face of incoming attacks. I have seen it work over and over again enough times to guarantee results with this one drill alone.

When performing the Five Kick drill I will use what I call "token blocks", tapping rather than moving my partner's kicks so as to not disturb the flow of the drill. As with the Five punch drill, this is done in a back and forth manner. A key point is that this drill is done smoothly and without force. I have found that people have difficulty defending against kicks and this is a great drill to handle that difficulty.

The combination Five Attack drill done back and forth.

I stress learning defense right at the beginning. The purpose of defense is, at its simplest function, is to make your opponent miss. He strikes at you aiming to land his blow. You do something that makes him miss. Pure and simple. How do you know what he is going to throw? You read his body telegraph. How do you do that? You use your Monitoring. Once again, the definition of the word monitor is "…to watch something, especially for a purpose." The purpose for this use is to see what attack is coming at you so that you can handle it effectively.

Okay, so let's spar…

At this stage of the game, remember that we are still working on how to learn on how to spar. We are not even at the stage of free-sparring yet. We begin with development sparring. In development sparring what you really need is a partner who will let you "win". It is usually in this type of training where I really stress understanding the definition of the word 'partner':

- A person who takes part in an undertaking with another or others

- Someone who you do a particular activity with

- One that is united or associated with another or others in an activity or a sphere of common interest, especially

What does a partner do? A partner works with you to achieve a goal. Works with you, not against you. When working on the block and counter defense your partner must be willing to be the loser. Otherwise, sparring becomes a game of winning and losing and this, even in controlled or playful situations, begins to resemble a fight or a competitive match. When working on sparring development, you're not there yet. Have patience. Play the development game.

In the beginning, I limit the attacker to straight punch and front kick and here is the defining rule: if my partner blocks incorrectly, I am moving too fast. Note that the error was not his, but mine. I was the person who did something wrong, not him. My moving too fast or too hard shifted my partner from cause to effect. Most people who begin free-sparring start out at effect to begin with. The key is to get from being an effect to being cause and then remaining there. Slow, extremely restricted free-sparring is the most effective way I've found to teach any student how to free-spar. The instructor can add more attacks to be used as the student becomes comfortable with free-sparring.

Once you have learned how to handle attacks at a relaxed and non-threatening speed, it is time to go into the next step: unrehearsed back and forth with a partner. At this point I still limit the attacks to two moves, a front kick and straight punch. I do this to reduce the confusion factor inherent in beginning free-sparring. What is a confusion? It is simply too many misaligned particles going on. Here is a good example of confusion. Take a desk stacked with papers. Open the window and let the wind hit that stack. Now you have papers being blown all over the office while you watch. Now that is a confusion. Papers going every which way in front of your eyes. Free-sparring is a lot like that unless you limit the number of attacks along with the speed and power used with them.

Developmental combinations…

The developmental combinations I teach are very simple and are simply laid out. I set them up the same way I did in my first book: punch-punch, kick-kick, punch-kick, and kick-punch. I will outline in the next several pages the beginning developmental combinations you can use to begin your sparring training.

Development combinations - Punch-punch 1 - lead hand punch, rear hand punch.

Development combinations - Punch-punch 2 - lead hand back fist, rear hand body punch.

Development combinations - Punch-punch 3 - lead hand back fist, rear hand hook punch.

Development combinations - Punch-punch 4 - three step punch (against a retreat).

Developmental combinations - Kick-kick 1 - Rear leg front kick, set forward and front kick.

Developmental combinations - Kick-kick 2 - Rear leg front kick, set forward and round kick.

Developmental combinations - Kick-kick 3 - Rear leg round kick, same leg side kick.

Developmental combinations - Kick-kick 4 - Slide up side kick, spinning back kick.

Developmental combinations - Punch-kick 1 - Step forward rear punch, rear leg front kick.

Development combinations - Punch-kick 2 - Step forward rear hand punch, rear leg round kick.

Developmental combinations - Punch-kick 3 - Step forward back fist, lead leg side kick.

Developmental combinations - Punch-kick 4 - Rear leg step forward and punch, spinning back kick.

Developmental combinations - Kick-punch 1 - Front kick, straight punch.

Development combinations - Kick-punch 2 - Step forward rear leg round kick, back fist.

Developmental combinations - Kick-punch 3 - Slide up side kick-back fist.

Development combinations - Kick-punch 4 - Spinning back kick, rear hand straight punch.

Linking combinations…

An important note regarding combinations is how to link your moves together. When throwing a combination, whether it is composed of only two moves or many more, a key point to make is to link your moves together rather than throw them one at a time. What I mean by this is it's all too common for a beginner to do one move, reset to his guard and then throw another move and so on. This unfortunately creates gaps in your offense in which your partner can insert a counter strike. How you want to develop a combination is that the end of your striking portion of any attack is the beginning of your next one. As you retract your first attack, another one is on the way. This creates a link from one strike to the next.

Note how there is no attack following right behind the front kick. This is an unlinked combination.

As this combination is not linked, she can hit me during my reset.

Linking your moves together closes all the gaps in your offense and makes it hard to counter you.

Punch delivers as leg retracts

Styles of Free-Sparring...

To keep the student from being completely bored when learning how to free-spar, I have come up with several different developmental methods of sparring one can use:

Back & Forth Sparring – You and your partner take turns attacking. This is the first style of free-sparring I have beginning students do. Back and forth sparring takes the confusion out of who is the attacker and who is the defender. This style of sparring is marked by the student putting together combinations of basic hand and foot attacks accompanied with footwork. This type of sparring is used to develop the student's ability to throw and block combination attacks. Evasion is not used much at this level.

It doesn't get any more complex than what you see in the above photos. She attacks at me with two to four attacks and then she backs out. I attack at her and she blocks. We take turns, back and forth, back and forth. The only thing that might be unpredictable is what she or I will throw. That's all. Smooth, safe and relaxed is what you are looking for in this style of sparring.

Balance Sparring – You repeat on the opposite side what you just did on the starting side, all within the same group of motions. Example: you throw a right leg front kick followed by a left hand straight punch. Your next turn at attacking you would throw the opposite, a left leg front kick followed by a right hand straight punch. In this type of free-sparring one develops both sides of the body equally, an important factor in the Super Dan Method.

In the above illustration I do a very simple round kick followed by a straight punch action. Note that when I finish the punch, I withdraw my lead foot in order to give me room to repeat the round kick with the other leg. Once I am done with my balance action, it is her turn. We both block without doing any counters. This drill is a simple but very effective way to train yourself to use both sides of your body for attack and defense.

Harmony Sparring – This is a very different style of free-sparring to train in. This is a light and controlled sparring where both partners are doing nothing which would interfere in any way with what the other person is trying do and, at the same time, his actions blending in with your own movements. Essentially you are both attacking to different targets simultaneously. You allow your partner to touch you with his kicks and punches and he allows you to the same. Doing this slowly with zero impact are the keys to this being a very good developmental style of sparring. You learn to watch your partner as you are hitting. You learn to relax when he is hitting at you. Relaxing in the face of your partner throwing techniques at you is one of the key skills you develop in the Super Dan Method. I call this "no block sparring" for the kids.

Important note: you are not looking to be able to win, score or counter attack your partner in any of these styles of sparring. These styles of free-sparring are baby steps. Why are these styles of free-sparing so important? Simple. These styles limit the confusion inherent in beginning free-sparring so that you can analytically process what is going on. You can observe and decide while in motion in a non-threatening situation. That last part is so important that I cannot stress it enough – *in a non-threatening situation*. With my students I'll

With my students I'll refer to this as "doing the dance". There's not a whole of lot of danger when you dance. There shouldn't be a whole lot of danger when you begin to spar.

Let's go back to the concept of cause and effect regarding beginning sparring. The concept of being "at cause" over what is happening in sparring is very important. If you use the "I hit you – you don't hit me" validation goal of free-fighting, where you successfully hit and keep from getting hit and you are in command of the situation, you are at cause. When you get hit by your opponent or partner, you lost your being at cause for that moment, you are now effect. The result of that is either you rise to the occasion or you tighten up, get frustrated, try too hard or even mentally concede (*"He's better than me. I'm having an off night."*). What happened was that under the standards you set up, you stopped being at cause over what was happening when you got hit. It goes through a downward spiral of action somewhat like this: *"I didn't want that to happen, they are now at cause and not me. I have got to get it back! I've got to try harder. It's not working!"* You see what I mean? This downward spiral is destructive to learning how to spar. Many students will quit before they get over this.

When you start out slowly with a zero confusion situation, you learn to be at cause and remain so. Your partner throws attacks at you which you can successfully block. You remain at cause. You do the same for your partner. He remains at cause. It's a win-win situation. When you use the harmony sparring style and *allow* your partner to touch/hit you (controlled, of course), you are not only being at cause when you hit, but also when you get hit. Now that is a different take on getting hit, isn't it? Cause over being hit. Let's examine that for a moment.

Harmony sparring provides a fascinating benefit. When you *allow* your partner to touch/hit you, you are taking your resistance to their attacks and throwing it out the window. You are freeing up the space between yourself and your opponent and in doing so, you are becoming more at cause over the situation. When you can allow yourself to be touch/hit by another, you are taking away all the negative significance attached to their attack. This is a way of mentally handling an attack. Give it freedom – do not resist its existence. Allow it to come at you. Finally, when you can allow it to be, to exist, to fly at you with destructive force and not reactively flinch, duck or hide, *then you can do whatever you want with it without being tense.* Then you can *respond* rather than blindly react. Block it, let it hit you, let it fall short, anything. Freeing their attack up will free you up. Resist their attack and that resistance will tighten you.

In the long run, allowing your partner to touch (touch, not impact) you with their hit will:
1. Desensitize/deactivate the flinch response
2. Allow you to relax enough to cleanly observe it coming at you
3. Allow you to use the defense you want because you are now mentally relaxed.

Relax...
You will see this word often enough and you might wonder how relaxed is relaxed? Well, relaxed is Tai Chi relaxed. That's how relaxed you should be when you first learn to spar. You don't necessarily need to go that slowly, but you should be that relaxed. This will smooth out your combinations while taking any appearance of dangerousness out of them. Relax. You will have enough time later on to go fast and hard.

Adding evasion into your basic sparring...

I went over evasion in the section on Monitoring and I'll go over it again here. Once you can do this easily and relaxedly, I now add in body motion monitoring so that you can use some defensive footwork in your developmental sparring. Using body motion monitoring you watch your partner's shoulders, not his hands. This is key for evasion. You move right when you spot the tell-tale motion of your partner's shoulders. A huge mistake to make is to wait until you recognize the commitment of your partner. That is way too late, especially if your partner has a quick take off. You will get hit that way.

One of the biggest mistakes in using evasion/distance as your defense is to overdo it. Any target your opponent is hitting at is relatively small. The target isn't a 3 by 3 foot sized target. It's small. Therefore your evasion doesn't have to be a large movement. It can be short and sweet. Once again, "Aim small, miss small." The target your opponent is aiming at is small, so you make him miss small.

Another mistake is using evasion to camouflage a flinch. This is done more often than one would expect. I will teach blocking first to train how to handle the attack before I teach how to make one miss. I feel that is a better progression. In competition, I was terrific at making my opponent miss but it came out of a fear of getting hit. There is nothing wrong with not wanting to get hit, however, it can lead to never developing a workable defense. A workable defense must include how to protect yourself if you get caught in a corner or somewhere you can't readily step away from. Develop your blocking, parrying, and covering defenses and they will not fail you if you can't step away.

The above being said, here are some example steps you can use in your training which will come in handy later in this book.

Slide back is a simple one-two step beginning with an extension of the back leg. You step back with the back foot and then follow with your lead foot backwards to resume your original guard position. This creates enough distance for your opponent to miss.

The angle step is a lead leg step forwards at a 45 degree angle. This will get you off of the Connection Line.

Maintain your alignment when angle stepping so that you can handle any possible follow up attack from your partner.

A spin-off combines a rotation to your rear with a follow up step to make a 90 degree step to the side.

A side step is a lead step directly to the side followed by the rear foot.

Any time you use stepping as a defense option, you want to make sure that you do not pull yourself out of position to continue your defense or counter attack. Maintaining your alignment with your partner is of paramount importance.

In the above photos you can see that I have compromised my position with my defensive step.

When you maintain your alignment with your partner, you will be able to protect yourself if or when your partner tracks your movement and continues their attack.

Maintaining your alignment while executing a slide back.

Maintaining your alignment while executing an angle step.

Free-Sparring Approaches
Direct Approach...
Okay, enough of the conceptual and back to the physical. What the heck do you do when learning free-fighting? How do you approach your partner? How do you learn to put your moves together to begin with? Without a frame of reference, it will be a mass of confusion. So, to ease the confusion I have split up basic free-sparring into two categories, direct and indirect approach.

Direct approach is straight-forward action with no deception involved. You move from point 'A' to point 'B' without any tricks or deceptions. This is learned first. Indirect approach is where you begin to use deceptive tactics and learned second. When learning your basics you have already begun to learn a direct approach – single move hitting. This is called Direct Attack. As you became proficient in this, you learned to put your moves together in combinations. This is called Attack by Combination. We will get to the tactics and strategies involved in applying these in free-fighting later in the book. We are still in the development stage at this point. The first step is how to stand. The next step is learning how to construct combinations.

Preliminaries
How to stand...
It is often said that one must learn how to walk before you can run. It's the same in karate free-sparring or free-fighting. This is a book on learning how to use the Super Dan Method of Free-fighting. I will leave the learning of the basics of punching and kicking up to your own instructor. This is not a book on basics. I will, however, go over the guard or stance we use and why. There have been two differing schools of thought regarding offensive weapons. The Bruce Lee/Joe Lewis school of thought is to put your strong or dominant side forward and use those as your primary weapons of offense. A right handed person would use his right lead. This is a relatively quick way to develop a decent offense.

The other school of thought is the Chuck Norris ambidextrous approach, to develop both sides evenly. It wouldn't matter if you stood left or right foot forward because you could strike with either side. The Super Dan method uses the Norris method and it is from this viewpoint I teach my standing guard position. Much like a boxer, I teach my students to keep their hands up and face forward. From this position you have access to all your weapons of offense and defense.

The Bruce Lee/Joe Lewis positioning.

The Chuck Norris/Dan Anderson positioning.

A key point to the Super Dan positioning is to maintain alignment to your opponent when you move off of his Line of Attack.

Basic Footwork - Getting from point "A" to point "B"...

I went over in the section on Distancing how close you can stand to your opponent and still be safe. Footwork is how you get from outside of striking range to where you can hit your opponent. There are a number of offensive kinds of offensive footwork I teach to bring your attack to your sparring partner. I am not a believer in teaching only one or two kinds of footwork. People come in all sizes. Some are naturally quick and some are not. Ever since the Bruce Lee phenomenon, there has been a lot of emphasis on being explosive and "bridging the gap" with explosive speed and so on. Joe Lewis was a prime exponent of using explosive footwork to bridge the gap in his point fighting career. Explosive footwork has been taken as gospel ever since. There, however, is a problem with this. Bruce Lee was roughly 135 lbs., in the best shape of his life and had "fast twitch muscles". Joe Lewis was roughly 190 lbs., in the best shape of his life and had fast twitch muscles. Being quick and sudden comes naturally to someone who has fast twitch muscles. What about someone who is 220 lbs. and out of shape? How about a housewife who has never done any physical sport in her life? What about the normal guy who doesn't have 3-5 hours daily to train? What if you don't have fast twitch muscles? To demand explosive entry of every student of karate is not realistic. The explosive speed that is so popularized is not natural to many people training in martial arts. To condemn someone to one method of stepping which will never be natural to them is condemning them to defeat. You don't need explosive speed to bridge the gap. There are other methods of offensive footwork available to all kinds of students. The Super Dan Method takes all this into consideration. I am going to show both explosive footwork and methods of entry which do not need speed to cross the gap. There are more ways than one to skin a cat.

Slide Forward consists of a simple 1-2 stepping pattern. You reach with your lead foot and follow step with your rear foot. This is a medium speed method of stepping.

Two key points in using the Slide Forward are: 1. Coordinate your strike with your lead foot step so that it lands upon arrival and 2. step, not drag your rear foot forward as you finish the step.

A Slide Back is the reverse action of the Slide Forward. The rear foot steps first followed by the lead foot.

A Lunge is a quick burst version of the Slide Forward. Note the bend of the rear leg for take off.

Knees bent for quick take off

The Lunge Kick is characterized by the rear leg pushing off just as the lead leg raises to kick. This is a very quick action but needs to be in close range to work effectively.

Heel begins to raise off the floor...

Rear leg pushes as the kick begins to launch

Rear leg hops forward as the kick fires

The Grapevine Step is a cross leg step for delivering the round kick, side kick and hook kick. You cross step in front of your kicking leg for the round kick and behind the kicking leg for the side and hook kicks.

Beside the lead foot

Behind the lead foot

Note: the farther your opponent is away from you, the larger your cross step will need to be.

The Slide Up is where you draw your fear foot up to your lead foot in preparation for the kick.

A Skip Kick is the quick version of the Slide Up kick. A key point of this type of step is that your stepping foot takes the place of the kicking foot. Your kick should be firing as your rear foot lands.

Feet change in mid air

The preceding series of footwork types are for when you are at range or slightly inside of range. The Lunge, Lunge kick and Skip kick are all inside range footworks. They are short, quick and snappy movements in which you trade distance covering ability for speed. The Grapevine steps are more for when you are on the Critical Distance Line. The Slide forward can be used at either distance position, although it is better for when you are inside range.

Let's go over what to do if your opponent likes to keep a longer range than you want. The thing I have found over the years is that your opponent never wants to cooperate. You will want to kick and he will block it. You want to fake him out and he won't bite. You will want to creep in and he'll want to stay away. So what do you do? In terms of footwork, what I do is change two aspect of the footwork:

1. Multiply the number of steps and

2. Slow the speed of my entry down

You will notice that the preceding steps are all single motions for going from A to B. An opponent keeping distance from you will negate that single action. You will need to double or triple up your steps to get to him. If your opponent keeps his distance, he will be able to see you coming at him. Okay, fine. This strategy works both ways. I will slow down my stepping (which I call Measured Footwork) so that I can easily see his counter. I can counter his strategy by using one of my own - *aggressive defense*. More on that later. I'll go over a couple of examples of compounding footworks to bridge the gap against someone who likes to keep distance on me. One key point to remember is don't be impatient. Don't rush it. When you do the multiple steps, you will get there.

The Double Step begins as a Slide Forward but the key difference is that you bring your rear foot forward ahead of your lead foot to cover more distance.

The Slide Up-Step Through.

A Multiple Shuffle or Multiple Slide Up is a very effective way to measure your speed as you cross the gap.

Aggressive Defense is where you measure your forward speed so that if your opponent attacks as you come in, you can see it in time and be able to block and counter that attack.

A key point to the success of the Aggressive Defense is to keep moving forward as you execute the block or parry.

There is one more measured approach that is a favorite of mine. I call it the "Zombie Walk". When I do the Zombie Walk, I move in a lower pace than the multiple footworks. I just do a series of steps where I creep forward at my opponent. As I do this, I shield my body with my arms so that any kick or punch he might throw at me will be absorbed by my cover. One thing I have found out over the many years is that people are impatient. People are unwilling to wait. This was one of my greatest assets in tournament fighting. I was a defensive fighter. It was no problem for me to wait for nearly the entire match for my opponent to make a mistake. When I do the Zombie Walk, I just slowly come at my opponent knowing that at some point he will not be able to stand it and will fire an attack at me. It works every time.

There are several key points to its success. The first is to Monitor. You must watch your opponent closely so that you recognize what he is throwing at you. I've gone over that extensively in section two of this book. The second is to cover his target effectively. Let's go over that point now. There is one karate position that I use to do what I call "Cover Monitoring". It is a variation of the position that Joe Lewis and Bill Wallace used when they fought both in karate and full contact fighting.

Joe Lewis (left) vs Chuck Norris (right)   *Bill Wallace*

My variation on this is that I keep my rear hand up higher to cover against any shots to the head. One thing to keep in mind is that this cover position is a mobile one, ready to move to cover up against a strike.

Note how I can move my arms from my basic position (left) to different points to cover up targets.

Here are a couple of examples of using Cover Monitoring against a jab and hook punch.

Cover Monitoring against a front kick and round kick. Note how I close the guard against the front kick.

Cover Monitoring against a round kick and hook kick. Using my rear hand to cover to my inside.

An example of the Zombie Walk. I just slowly move in until my opponent gets frustrated and fires off an attack. The moment the attack hits my guard is the moment I counter attack.

There is a tactic in boxing that will help you execute the Zombie Walk successfully called "cutting off the ring". What you do not want to happen is for your opponent lead you around or make you chase them. You want to control the situation. If you get an opponent who likes to move and circle around, what you do is this: move toward them in a relaxed and steady fashion. When they step to the left side, you step to your right side with them. If they step to the other side, you do the same. You mirror the direction of their movement. Don't worry that you are not progressing toward them as you step to one side or the other. You are cutting off their circling and that is what you want. When they step back you resume your forward movement. Unless you are outside in an open field, you will corner them or back them into a wall or they will attack you out of frustration. Either way you are now engaged. The key on this is to be patient. When being tracked down like this, one gets a feeling of inevitability. Good. That's how you want them to feel. It takes them out of their game.

Cutting off the ring: In the above example, she attempts to circle to her left. As she steps, I step to my right and cut her off. She steps back and I continue my pursuit.

All together now…

Now that you know why I stand the way I do, let's get back to the subject of combinations. So what is a combination? For free-sparring purposes, a combination is a series of kicks and punches linked into one continual action. The key words are "linked" and "action". A combination is not a bunch of moves strung together. A combination of moves must be linked together so that the series of actions flow together. The easiest way to describe this is in the diagram below.

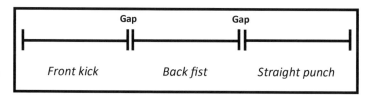
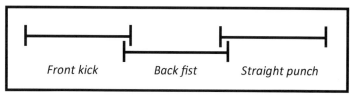

Note that in the first diagram the attacks are singular, unconnected actions. This is how a beginner usually throws a combination. He'll do the first strike. Reset. Do the second one. Reset. And finish with the third one and reset again. In a combination that is connected, the beginning of the second action is at the tail end of the first one. That is crucial to maintaining a flow of action. You don't complete the first attack fully and then fire off the next. This will leave a gap between your strikes that an opponent can take advantage of. A simple example of this would be you are in your fighting stance and throw a punch. You retract your punch and reset back to your guard position. Then you throw the second punch. This creates a series of actions that consists of "something-nothing-something". A good counter-fighter will hit you during the "nothing" phase. The reset stage is a great time to get hit.

For a combination to flow, you begin the second attack at the final stage of the first one. This is usually during its retraction stage. In using the above example, you would throw your first punch. At the very beginning of its retraction your second punch begins. Note that when you do this there is no gap, no point where you are doing nothing. A combination attack is a continuous flow of attacks much like pouring water from a pitcher on someone's head. It doesn't stop and take a pause somewhere in the middle. It just keeps coming. It doesn't matter if you throw a two move combination or a ten move combination. The flow is the same.

This is the second stage of free-sparring development, getting from the one move stage to putting moves together. Learning to throw combination attacks is a great way to increase coordination and develop a flow of motion. Go back to the section where I delineate the developmental combinations and you will see that they all connect into one flowing action. Work them. Drill them until your body has the feel of delivering a continuous series of actions in one overall flowing motion. We will get to how to use your combinations in free-sparring and later free-fighting soon. The important thing is to get your actions strung together first.

Direct Approach - Defense…

Defensively, there are a couple of options to work on as you learn how to free-spar. The first is to be able to continuously defend against the incoming attacks. Done relaxedly, you will develop your ability to monitor your partner's actions. Again, I must emphasize the importance of the striker starting out slowly and building up speed and power gradually. This is to work on the defender's ability to face incoming shots without a flinch reaction. Just as you develop a familiarity with handling attacks being thrown one at a time, now you work on developing the same familiarity with handing two, three, four attacks and so on.

I teach both defending while standing still as well as defending and retreating. As long as the retreat is not a disguised flinch reaction, using distance as an aid to your defense is a good tactic. One point to make right here is that when you practice evasion as a tactic, maintain your structure and alignment as you do so. Otherwise you leave yourself open to get hit and cut off your possibility to counter.

Once you feel comfortable enough to watch kicks and punches coming at you and blocking them, you can handle multiple attacks thrown at you. The next defensive option I teach is to block and hit back. There is a key point I stress in this option – you want to hit back after your first block or parry. A well done combination attack is like a snowball rolling downhill. It gathers momentum as each attack follows the next. Block and counter is a defense designed to *halt* the combination before it gathers momentum.

A huge mistake is to wait until your partner is finished with his combination attack before you counter strike. This is way too late and could end up getting you hit. If you wait until your partner is done hitting, he may have enough momentum to run right over you. Block and counter is used to stop your opponent just as he begins to go, before he builds up momentum. So, how do you do this?

You use a concept I call "touch trigger". You begin your counter attack just *as* your defense touches your partner's strike. This follows the same cycle of action as an attack combination sequence. Your counter attack is linked with your defense, but goes much sooner.

One of the big mistakes in doing this defensive approach is to wait until your block or parry completes before you throw your counter. Timing wise, this allows your opponent to slip in his next attack and keep you on the defensive. You want to insert your counter attack in between his series of attacks, preferably between attack numbers 1 & 2. Inserting your counter attack in between his series of attacks *interrupts* his flow of action.

Note that in the third photo above my counter attack is already firing as the block touches her attack.

Examples of touch trigger against kicks. In example one my counter attack begins as I clear the front kick. In example two my counter fires right when the round kick touches my guard.

Developing this ability to interrupt is of prime importance. Let's look at it this way. Have you ever been talking and the person who you're talking to cuts you off and starts yammering on and on about what they want to say? Then to top it off, you now can't get a word in edgewise? That is what you are developing with the touch trigger in your block and counter attack. You interrupt their action and then continue with an action of your own. Another way to depict this is in the photos below. A block and counter is an interruption, but it is more. It is "blow back". It is a flow reversal. Someone is coming at you and you reverse their direction, you reverse their intention. Their intention is to come forward and hit you. You shove that intention into reverse. There isn't much that is quite as unsettling as blow back phenomenon.

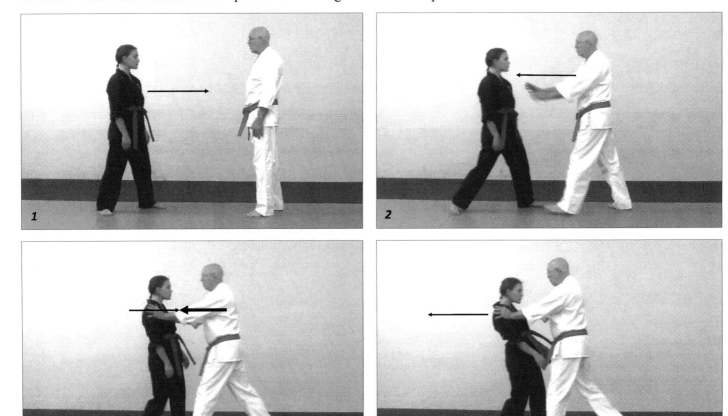

The above sequence represents what happens with a correctly executed block and counter. Her walking toward me represents her attack (1). My reach to her represents my defense (2). Her attack and my defense collide in the middle (3). My counter attack causes the mental disturbance I call blow back (4).

Free-sparring...

Now that you're relaxed with the training of direct offense and direct defense, it's time to put these skills to use, still in a limited fashion. It's time to play. Testing these skills are what you do in free-sparring. You test to see what you are good at and what you need work on. You cross the line of winning and losing in a limited fashion. This is the use of free-sparring. We're not in the realm of free-fighting yet. We'll get there. Let's now go over one more concept that you need to understand in order to free-spar now and later free-fight skillfully.

Intelligent Combinations - The next step in basic free-sparring...

Up till now you have been using developmental combinations to play with. Developmental combinations are easy to work your basic block and counter against. They are designed that way. Now it's time to become intelligent with what you're going to throw at your partner. Time for another definition, intelligent combination:

- An *intelligent combination* is one where each attack opens up a hole in your partner's defense. Each succeeding attack continues to open up holes in your partner's defense. If your partner has any hesitations in his counters, this type of offense will work very well for you.

An intelligent combination should pull your partner out of position if he is not paying good attention or is slow on returning fire. You are not necessarily trying to win at this point but this will teach your partner to pay attention all the same. Following are examples of intelligent combinations that I teach in my school.

Punch combination 1: lead punch face, rear punch body, lead punch body, rear punch face. This is a very simple intelligent combination but is a great example of opening a hole in your opponent's defense. I'll explain how it works.

On surface evaluation it looks like a very easy combination to defend against. It's just four punches. What could be so hard about that? Here is the thing that makes it work. You are manipulating your opponent's attention units. You are shifting them up and down very quickly, to quickly for him to adjust at full speed. At a medium speed it is no problem. At full speed it becomes a problem right away. A point to make here is that every combination (or fake for that matter - more on that coming up) is done with the idea that it will be done at full speed some time in the future. When you are learning any action, start out in this order: correctly, fluidly and then with speed and power. Okay back to the combination. Check out the photo sequence below. It is a dramatization of what occurs with your opponent's attention units when you do this combination.

The simplicity of the above combination is that my first punch draws her attention upwards. My second punch pulls it down sharply. The third punch sticks it there by firing another punch at the same target. The fourth one lands. At full speed you may land as early as the second action. It all depends on how fast your opponent is able to perceive and shift attention.

When throwing combinations, there is a good rule of thumb I use as regards to targeting. I split the body up into four zones:

- Zone 1 - the head,
- Zone 2 - the chest,
- Zone 3 - the midsection and
- Zone 4 - the groin and below.

I *never* target two zones next to each other such as Zone 1-Zone 2. I have found that one's attention can easily span two zones. I strike two zones apart. In the above sequence I am striking the zones in this order: 1-3-3-1. You will see in the following intelligent combinations the same pattern

This next combination is another great example of jacking around your opponent's attention units as you not only shift them up and down but side to side as well.

This is a simple five move combination: lead hand back fist, rear punch to the body, lead hand back fist, round punch (hook punch, palm hook, ridge hand - it doesn't matter what kind of round punch you use) and lead hand punch to the body. Executed rapid fire this combination sends your opponent's attention units in all directions as shown on the next page.

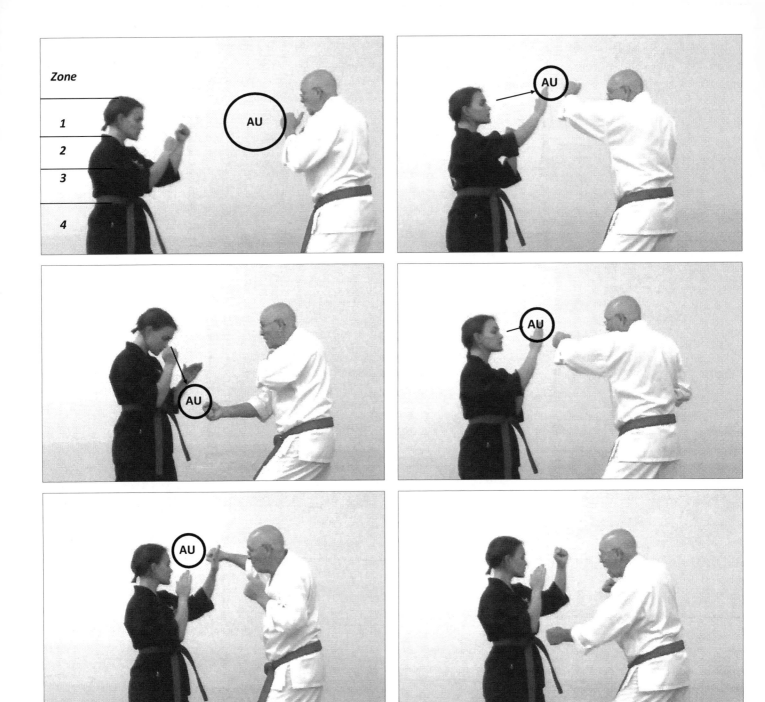

Do you see what I mean by manipulating your opponent's attention units? Once you grasp this simple concept, you will be able to formulate all sorts of intelligent combinations for yourself. Remember, as you do this, that the definition of a combination is two or more attacks each intending to hit. Don't get into the habit of just tossing out your first or second attack in the hopes that your opponent will pay attention to them. Make each attack real. Use your footwork to get you within reach of your opponent and execute each action so that it will go to the target. That will get your opponent's attention for sure.

The first intelligent kick combination I learned was this one - the rear leg front kick which transfers into a round kick. You draw the attention down to expose the head for the follow up kick (zone 4 - zone 1).

During my competitive years, this was a favorite of mine - the shuffle up low-high round kick (zone 4 - zone 1).

This is a basic intelligent combination that anyone can execute. Note that my follow up punch goes right when she blocks (zone 3 - zone 1). . This is a sort of offensive touch trigger.

This was another favorite action of mine - skip round kick low followed by a back fist to the head.

Styles of Free-Sparring…

Now you're ready to play a little bit. Let's play. I will repeat the three initial styles of sparring for your reference.

Back & Forth Sparring – This is where you and your partner take turns attacking. This is the first style of free-sparring I have beginning students do. Back and forth sparring takes the confusion out of who is the attacker and who is the defender. This style of sparring is marked by the student putting together combinations of basic hand and foot attacks accompanied with footwork. This type of sparring is used to develop the student's ability to throw and block combination attacks. Evasion is not used much at this level.

Balance Sparring – You repeat on the opposite side what you just did on the starting side all within the same group of motions. Example: you throw a right leg front kick followed by a left hand straight punch. Your next turn at attacking you would throw the opposite, a left leg front kick followed by a right hand straight punch. You switch stance positions from left lead to right lead while doing this. In this type of free-sparring one develops both sides of the body equally, an important factor in the Super Dan Method.

Harmony Sparring – This is a very different style of free-sparring to train in. This is a light and controlled sparring where both partners are doing nothing which would interfere in any way with what the other person is trying do and, at the same time, his actions blending in with your own movements. Essentially you are both attacking to different targets simultaneously. You allow your partner to touch you with his kicks and punches and he allows you to the same. Doing this slowly with zero impact are the keys to this being a very good developmental style of sparring. You learn to watch your partner as you are hitting. You learn to relax when he is hitting at you. Relaxing in the face of your partner throwing techniques at you is one of the key skills you develop in the Super Dan Method. I call this "no block sparring" for the kids.

Important note: you are *still* not looking to be able to score or counter attack your partner in any of these styles of sparring. These styles of free-sparring are baby steps, development tools. You are working with motion (yours and his) and turning it into co-motion (yours and his together). Have the patience to do sparring this way to fully familiarize yourself with moving with your partner.

Lastly, as you become more and more familiar with your sparring, now you can add more and more punching and kicking techniques until you can spar fluidly and relaxedly. Once you can do that, now you add in your block and counter moves you've learned. At this point you are tipping over into a quasi free-fighting mode but not quite yet. At this point you are still being mechanical and not tactical. You are still working on how to put together all the things you have learned. Your combinations are now of the intelligent type. Your block and counter is becoming more and more touch trigger.

Once you can do that with a relaxed frame of mind, you're ready. Let's free-fight!

Section Four:

Application

144

Let's Free-fight!

When you are at the point of your training where you feel totally relaxed about striking at your partner and your partner striking at you, you are ready to free-fight. This will take as long as it takes to develop this and varies broadly from person to person. Just like learning how to free-spar, learning how to free-fight is taken in gradual steps where you start out slowly and add speed and power as you develop.

So, what is free-fighting? Free-fighting is limiting combat fighting down to an agreed upon set of rules.

Free-fighting is dueling.

This is either competitive freestyle or fight training in a school. There are all sorts of competitive freestyle: point karate, continuous karate, Olympic taekwondo, kickboxing, Thai boxing, san shou/san da, mixed martial arts (cage fighting). These are all forms of free-fighting. Yes, you are going for the win, yet you are governed by rules. There are certain things you are allowed and not allowed to do. Yes, you can get hurt doing this but at the same time, it can be stopped by an official. This could be considered as sport combat or game fight. I do not mean this as any kind of slight but to define it for what it is. I played competition for many, many years and I got very good at the game. Yes, the game. I do not believe for a moment that it is real combat. Fight training in a school is also limited both by the degree of contact or impact one can make and take. This is about as close to fighting as you can safely get. You can drill the viewpoint of win/lose in free-fighting.

Willingness to lose and willingness to win are attitudes you will have to develop in order to become proficient in free-fighting.

In free-fighting your goal is to win, to hit and not get hit, to foil your opponent's tactics and strategies for hitting you. This is also a game, especially in the beginning, albeit with a different purpose. Here is where your attitude needs to be especially important. Initially you must be *willing to lose*. Yes, willing to lose. Just as any learning process you will make mistakes. How many mistakes did you make learning how to drive? To use a computer? To cook? To play a video game? Lots! Well, learning how to free-fight is no different. If you are willing to make mistakes and lose in the beginning, your self-esteem will not lower. I saw this again and again in tournament fighting. Some guy would be really bummed at losing a match or several tournaments in a row and after a while, he would "lose interest" in going to them or even in karate itself. What happened? He felt like he couldn't do it so he moved on. He put so much importance on winning that he wasn't willing to go through the usual learning process which included losing. Instead, he took it personally, decided he wasn't any good and bolted. You must be willing to make mistakes and lose in the process and not take it personally. That is the first attitude you need.

The second attitude you will need is being *willing to win*. That's a funny one because I have never had that problem, but surprisingly enough, many students do. I have found it quite odd that the majority of people I have taught are more willing to be hit than hit someone. I put this down to the fact that people are basically good and don't want to cause another harm. This is easily handled by putting body armor (I will use the taekwondo chest protectors for this) on students and let them bang away. It seems the protection of the armor frees up the student to hit another.

Alright, how do we go about this winning business, anyway? Let's proceed.

Free-fighting Approaches…

Back in the 1970s, Bruce Lee came out with what he called the "angles of attack". This was one of the first breakdowns of different ways one could initiate the offense at his opponent. To clarify the term, 'angle' in this sense means:

- A particular way of approaching or considering an issue or problem

After Bruce Lee passed away in the early 1970s, Lee's number one student, Dan Inosanto, further clarified the five offensive approaches to free-fighting in the prevailing magazines of the day. Two premier point fighters, Joe Lewis and Al Dacascos, further delineated these to include three types of defensive fighters (blockers, jammers, and runners). In my first book, *American Freestyle Karate: A Guide To Sparring*, I expanded on the defensive types to a fuller description of the defensive approaches to free-fighting. The five offensive and seven defensive approaches became the bulk of that book and they are the base of my tactical approaches. They were new back in 1980 and remain valid to this day.

Simply stated the offensive approaches are:

- Direct attack (a singular attack intending to land)

- Attach by combination (two or more attacks each intending to land)

- Indirect attack (an attack which has a preliminary diversion such as a feint, leg sweep, etc.)

- Attack by trapping (an attack preceded by an immobilization of a limb in order to prevent a successful defense)

- Attack by drawing (this is leaving an opening for your attacker to attack so that as he strikes at it, he leaves open a target on himself and you hit the opening)

The defensive approaches are:

- Hit when your opponent changes (when your opponent shifts weight, changes stance, drops his lead hand, etc. (this can also be categorized as an offensive timing point)

- Hit as the ranges cross (this is stepping forward and hitting your opponent as he begins his attack)

- Hold your position and hit (you counter strike just as your opponent does his attack)

- Simultaneous block and hit (you block and hit at the time)

- Block and hit (this is blocking and counter-striking in a one-two action)

- Block (this is blocking your opponent's attacks with no counter attack of your own)

- Evade and counter (this is moving out of the way of the attack and then counter-striking)

- Evade (this is moving out of the way of the attack without counter-striking)

That is the shopping list. Now let's go over each one beginning with the Offensive Approaches.

Offensive Approaches

Direct Attack...

- Definition: A singular attack with the intention to hit

It doesn't get any more simple than that. You launch one strike and hit with it. Obviously there are five factors that will play into your Direct Attack being effective. The first is your *when* to launch the attack. Go back to the section on Timing and review when to launch your attack. The examples listed there will give you a start as to when you want to launch your attack against your opponent. The second is Distancing. A Direct Attack is most effective when you launch it from inside the critical distance line. If you can sneak inside the critical distance line the distance you have to cover will be shorter and your quick burst will be harder to defend against. The third factor is what is called *initial move*. Initial Move is synchronizing your entry footwork and your attack to occur at the same time. If you throw your attack after your entry footwork, you run the hazard of getting hit by your opponent when you arrive. If you throw your attack ahead of your entry it will fall short. Initial Move is crucial to the success of your Direct Attack. The forth factor is quickness. Quickness is degree of sudden motion. Quick is not speed. Speed is raw velocity. Quick is how sudden you go from no motion to motion. I have seen many fighters who were not quick. Once they got going, they were very fast and hard to overcome. Fighters who hit you right off the bat without being detected are quick. The fifth factor is being committed. Full commitment to your Direct Attack will enable you to cover the range and hit your opponent. A phrase that really sums this up is one from several time world champion Ray McCallum: *"Technique to target."* It doesn't get any simpler than that. Here are some examples of Direct Attack that have served me well.

Lead hand strike - I am prepared to take off and am slightly inside her range (1). I use Initial Move so that my lead hand and lead foot move at the same time (2). My strike lands as I cover the distance between the two of us (3&4).

Direct Attack using the lunging rear hand punch. Note the use of Initial Move.

Lead leg angle kick to the groin was another favorite of mine.

A key point to the Super Dan positioning is to maintain alignment to your opponent when you move off of his Line of Attack.

The preceding were simple examples of Direct Attack. It is the simplest of the five offensive approaches. Remember that Direct Attack needs five factors for it to work:

- Timing
- Distancing
- Initial Move
- Quickness
- Commitment.

Attack by Combination...

I've gone over the subject of combinations in the preceding section. I define a combination as:

- Two or more attacks each intending to hit

A combination needs the same factors as a Direct Attack to make it work. One of the saving graces of Attack by Combination is that if you miss your first shot *and* your opponent has not countered you, you can still hit with your follow up strikes. Go back over the sections on developmental and intelligent combinations to refresh yourself on the basics of them and then investigate the following examples.

Note that in this simple shuffle up front kick/two punches follows the dictum of not hitting two zones next to each other.

Skip side kick followed by back fist to the head.

Rear leg round kick followed by a back fist to the head.

A liability of an incorrectly done Attack by Combination is to attempt to chase down your opponent with the techniques alone. It is very easy to step away from kicks and punches without covering the distance first.

A key action to use against a retreating opponent is to use your footwork to cover the distance before you deliver your attacks. If they run, cover the distance first and strike second.

Indirect Attack...

- Indirect (definition) - deviating from a straight line; not going straight to the point

Direct Attack and Attack by Combination are very straight forward approaches with no hint of deviousness in them. Indirect Attack is the opposite. With Indirect Attack you are playing with your opponent's attention. You want his attention on one thing or area while you hit another area. That is the simplicity of it. A favorite example way to explain Indirect Attack is in the photos below. I'll use humor to get the point across.

When middleweight boxer Rocky Graziano was knocked out by Sugar Ray Robinson, his comment to the press was, *"I shoulda zigged when I zagged."* With Indirect Attack, that is the idea of what you are doing to your opponent.

Faking/feinting...

The terms 'faking' and 'feinting' are often used interchangeably but the 'feint' is the proper term. Let's go over definitions first (Oxford dictionary).

- Fake: to trick or deceive (an opponent) by making a fake (often followed by out):
  The running back faked out the defender with a deft move and scored.

- Feint: a movement made in order to deceive an adversary; an attack aimed at one place or point merely as a distraction from the real place or point of attack; *the feints of a skilled fencer.*

Technique fake...

I have used the word "fake" for so long that I will continue to use it in this text. What is a technique fake? It is an unfinished technique because your opponent reacted. How does an unfinished technique cause a reaction? Well, what does a real technique contain? Speed, power, aim and intent. A fake must contain the same. One of the biggest mistakes beginners make is to fake the fake, to not make it real. Nothing looks less realistic than a half hearted attempt at a technique and no skilled fighter is going to fall for something like that. Look at like this. A fake is a real technique that you changed your mind about in order to throw something else. So what made you change your mind? Your opponent's reaction. Why did he react? Because something was coming he was going to get hit by. That is a fake!

Leading centers fake...

A second kind of faking is when you use body motion to hint that you are going to throw a technique. Leading center fakes consist of use of the shoulder, hips or head to give off a tell-tale sign of a technique being thrown. Leaning forward with the shoulder appears like a back fist is coming. Rolling your hips toward your opponent shows that a kick is on its way. This is what you are giving your opponent a look at. A smart opponent is looking for these kinds of tell-tale signs. This is something you can use against him.

Commitment fakes...

The third category of fakes that I teach is Commitment fakes. A commitment fake is where you take off with a short burst, covering 6 inches at the most. This replicates an explosive take off. By going only 6 inches you halt out of your opponent's striking range. Your opponent watches for nothing but a committed entry. He doesn't watch leading centers or techniques. He watches for you to take off full bore. I discovered this one while training with the late Larry Kelly. We were at Greg Silva's school and I noticed that his fighters didn't react to the kinds of fakes I was doing at the time, but every time I attacked, they nearly jumped out of their skins. I thought that was interesting so I decided to give something a try. I was attacking from the Critical Distance Line. I did my first Commitment fake and got my partner to jump. Then I checked something. How was his knowledge of range. I snuck inside of range to see if he'd react. He didn't. Interesting! Here is when I formed another Super Dan strategy - check to see if my opponent reacts to a quick burst.

Faking and Opponent Reactions...

Here is an interesting question for you: How can you tell what kind of fake your partner will react to? This was an interesting dilemma of mine for many years. I made a major breakthrough when I was training with a friend of mine, Fred King. Fred would use leading center fakes (movement of the shoulders or hips telegraphing the technique) on me. I would use techniques fakes (partially executed techniques to get him to respond) on him. Neither one of us were falling for the other. He would pop his hip at me or make a motion with his shoulder and I would wonder why he was doing that. I'd fake a technique at him and he would just stand there waiting for me to come in. I couldn't get him to flinch. One day it hit me out of the blue. Here is what the problem was. Neither of us were trained in the other's way of thinking. I didn't know the concept of leading centers and he wasn't taught to watch techniques. As far as I was concerned, he was just jerking his body and that meant nothing to me. He never fell for my technique fake because he could tell by my lack of shoulder movement that I was not committing to the attack.

This lead to my major breakthrough on feints:

YOUR FAKES MUST PARALLEL THE EDUCATION OF YOUR OPPONENT.

Fascinating! I then figured out how to safely test how your opponent has been educated. The funny thing is that he usually never figures out how you are setting him up. I have found three predominant ways of faking. Most people will fall for at least one of them.

I have found that your opponent or partner will respond to:

- A commitment fake
- A body fake or
- A technique fake

The way I'll test someone is I'll check commitment fakes, body fakes, and techniques fakes, in that exact order. I go from safest to the most risky for me. When testing a commitment fake, you don't need to get into range of your partner. You pump him with the beginning of an entry step and see if he reacts. If he doesn't react, then I'll pop a hip or shoulder fake and see if he reacts. If no reaction there, I will try a technique fake. That will usually do it. If none of the above get a reaction, then I usually just attack with a combination or go on the defensive. It's rare that I don't get a reaction on one of the three. You can never fully know or assume what your partner is watching for. This method of figuring out how your partner will react has been very successful for me. I'll demonstrate some examples of the types of fakes in the following pages for you beginning with how to cut short an attack followed by samples of some of the intelligent combinations.

A technique fake is a technique that is cut off from completion once a response is gotten. A key point is it should be done explosively and as real as possible otherwise it will look false and draw no reaction at all.

Technique samples above of techniques cut short: rear hand straight punch (1-4) and rear leg front kick (5-8).

Here are several faking options based on intelligent combinations. The rear punch fake-head punch (1-3), fake front kick low-high round kick (4-6) and the fake low round kick-head high round (7-9) all have one very important thing in common: the defense *never* touches the fake. You shift into your real attack while your opponent has his attention on the defense, not after he has completed his defense. If he is quick, he will be able to shift his attention to your real attack if you let him touch the fake.

I fake to zone 3 and follow up to zone 1.

She fakes to zone 4 and follows up to zone 1.

She fakes to zone 4 and follows up to zone 1.

Here are examples of shifting kick-kick numbers 3 (1-4) and 4 (5-8) from developmental combinations to fakes and follow ups.

More examples of the existing combinations being used as faking options.

Kick-punch 1

Kick-punch 3

Punch-kick 3

Punch-punch 2

Below are two examples of setting your opponent up with a lead hand punch. In the first example you draw attention upstairs and hit straight away (1-3). In the second example you draw their attention to the front of the face while striking to the side of the head with a hook punch (4-6).

In the preceding pages you now have more than enough examples as how to transform any of the kind of combinations I teach into fakes and follow ups. Now let's take up the subject of leading centers.

Leading center fakes...

A leading center is either a head, shoulder or hip that replicates the beginning of an attack. It is common knowledge in martial arts fighting that you cannot move the body forward at your opponent without moving the shoulders. Let's start with the shoulder fake. The shoulders moving forward or in any direction is a good way to tell if your opponent is coming at you. Quite often a fighter will overdo that motion without knowing it and then the telegraphing action becomes even more apparent. This is where using it as a fake comes in.

Broadly stated a shoulder coming forward telegraphs a lead hand punch of some sort coming at you.

The shoulder going down could mean a body punch while a shoulder going slightly upward could mean a back fist.

The hip rolling forward telegraphs a lateral kick such as side kick, round kick and hook kick, coming at you. The head and shoulders coming at you can telegraph a forward charge. A leading center action doesn't exactly tell you what is coming but will tell you that something is coming. For the purpose of faking, that is good enough.

Note the preparation of the hip prior to firing the round kick. If you are facing sideways, the forward action of the hip will be quite evident.

From a front facing position a hip turn is needed as well as pointing it towards the target.

Commitment fakes...

A commitment fake is the hardest one to perform as it involves:

- The entire body taking off at once,

- Exploding forward as fast as you can,

- Moving forward only about 6 inches and

- An immediate spring back to get back out to a safe range.

Done correctly, it gives your opponent the impression that you have taken off at him at full speed. You will get a reaction from most people doing this one. It can be done in conjunction with a technique fake as well.

Note how short of a distance I cover. This is why your explosiveness or suddenness of take off is so important. If this action is done softly or relaxedly, you will fool no one.

All right. Now you have the three types off faking actions in the Super Dan Method. What kinds of reactions are you looking for? You are looking at directional reactions. You want to see if your opponent will move backwards, forwards or stay still. This is what will tell you how your opponent has been educated. What he will do when he moves backward, forward or stand still will be covered more extensively in the section on Defensive Approaches. What you are looking for is how they will move when you move. This will give you a good clue as to their defensive orientation. If you are pretty sly about this, your opponent will never know that you are testing him. It has worked very well for me. It should for you.

When I test an opponent I will go in a very strict order based on what is safest for me. I test an opponent with:

- A commitment fake,
- A leading center fake and then
- A technique fake.

A commitment fake will get me in and out of range fast so that is the first one I do. If I get no reaction, I then do a leading center fake. That gets me into range but I am not so committed that I will get hit. If still no reaction then, I will do a technique fake. This gets me into range and if my opponent decides to strike at me I'll have to change gears and do some sort of aggressive defense action to keep from getting hit.

Testing a commitment fake - if my partner backs up there will be no need for me to spring backwards as she has increased the distance between us.

When executing a commitment fake, there are two possible responses from your opponent - backing up (1-4) or coming forward and attacking (5-8). As there is no attack with the fake you would not see a block.

A tactic I use when my opponent attacks as a response to a commitment fake is to halt short of her range of attack. As she now sees it was a false attack. She relaxes and that is when I counter attack.

I've found that one can expect all three responses from my opponent when I do a leading centers fake: retreat (1-4), stand still and block (5-8), or attack (next page).

If my opponent attacks as I do a leading center fake, I roll back and let it fall short.

One response from my opponent when I do a technique fake is to retreat.

Examples of my opponent backing off and blocking (1-4) or counter attacking (5-8)when I fake a technique.

So there you have it, the first of the Indirect Attack types, the art of faking/feinting. How do I deal with opponent responses? If someone backs off, I let them run. I do not go chasing down my opponent. Back in my competitive days, I was too good at taking advantage of my opponent's lack of patience and would make them pay if they chased me.

If someone blocks, that is fine. When a person blocks one area they leave another area open. That is where my real hit will go.

If they attack when I fake, I will take advantage of an interesting phenomenon. I will hit them on their energy drop. Here's how it works. For purposes of this explanation, my opponent is like a car idling. I start my fake and he steps on the gas and starts forward. I stop prematurely (in his eyes) so he stops. I hit him when he stops. He ramps up his energy just as he takes off. When he sees that I am not coming in, he stops coming in and his energy begins to drop. That is when I go. The trick is to have a split moment's hesitation between your fake and your follow up. (Cross reference this with the section on Broken Rhythm/Broken Flow on page 224)

When a person does a block in response, you want your real strike to land while they are still blocking and not when they have finished. With a counter attack response you do want them to finish their beginning of the counter. Energy up-energy down. Bang! They get hit. Drill these. Once you have the concepts down they are very simple to execute.

Leg taps/leg sweeps...
The second area of Indirect Attack deals with manipulating their attention units by physical touch. As I detailed in the beginning of the section on intelligent combinations, you want to play with your opponent's attention units. You want to move them and shift them around to your advantage. Using leg taps and leg sweeps are great ways of doing so. What differentiates a leg tap from a leg sweep? How do you know which to use in any given situation? The answer is very simple. How is your opponent standing? Look at the photo below.

Look at the way I am standing. My feet are too far apart for someone to leg sweep me successfully. My rear leg is positioned to use counter force against a sweep coming toward my front leg. For a leg sweep to be effective against me in this position, you would have to be a lot bigger than me to pull it off. I have successfully countered leg sweeps for years by having my stance to wide in a forward facing position. I did this, much to the surprise of my opponent, at an international competition in Cleveland, Ohio. In the warm up matches I was faced against a Japanese national or world champion (I can't remember which). During the match he came in at me with a leg sweep. I saw his set up for it and dropped my weight. His sweeping leg stopped dead on my planted leg as if he was kicking a tree trunk while I hit him with my counter punch. My legs were too wide for a leg sweep...but not for a leg tap which we'll get into now.

The idea of a leg tap is to swat your opponent's leg hard enough to get their attention. I have used a lead leg round kick to do this successfully. I have used the following two techniques successfully in national competitions. The first is the leg tap-back fist. I was down in Long Beach, California at the 1972 International Karate Championships. The lightweight black belt division was so big that they had to split it up into two rings. I was fighting Frank Wilson to see who would go to the finals that night. We had a tied score and the match went into overtime and whoever scored the first point won. This was the technique that put me into the evening finals and launched my nationally rated career.

Note that my back fist fires immediately on contact with the leg tap. I want to begin my strike up stairs as her attention goes down stairs (zone 4 - zone 1). This will ensure that my strike has the best possibility of landing.

This next example is one I seldom executed but I am glad I did at this particular tournament. I was at the 1979 Mid-America Diamond Nationals, one of the top rated tournaments in the late 1970s/early 1980s. I was fighting in the middleweight division again to see who would be fighting for first place in the evening finals. My opponent was David Deaton. I remembered Dave because he beat me in a match eight years before in my home region, the Pacific Northwest, and I never had a chance to even things up. We had both gotten a lot better in the ensuing eight years and here we were in overtime (again) in the semi-finals. This is the move I used to score on him to get into the finals. The odd thing is, I still don't know why I used this one as it was never a "go to" move for me. It just came out of thin air. I'm glad it did. I went on to win that match and the grand championship later on in the evening.

Above example of zoning (zone 4 - zone 1).

This next one is one of my favorite sucker moves. It is terrific for demoralizing an opponent because, on the surface, it looks like a really stupid move. What makes it work, however, is based on getting your opponent's attention units down to their hand when you pop it. The natural quickness of the back fist strike makes it easy to roll your strike over their hand right after the tap. A key point to mention is that you want to make the tap smack sharply against the hand to ensure that they feel it. It doesn't have to be a slam, but make it quick and sharp.

This really works best when your opponent allows you to get inside of range to begin with.

This last tapping action was a favorite action of a good buddy of mine, Robert Edwards. Still pictures don't really do this justice but I would be remiss if I didn't include it. Robert was one of the smoothest heavyweight fighters I have ever encountered. He would bounce rhythmically and as he did so, he would creep inside of your range. He'd move his hands back and forth during the bouncing. He would darn near mesmerize you with how smooth he was. At some point he'd be close enough to tap your lead hand and when he did, he would shift into a rear hand punch to your midsection.

Note that I tap her hand on the down bounce. This allows me to use the bend of my knees to shift forward for my punch.

This last example of Indirect Attack is one I chanced upon by accident. I was finding one day that my attempt at technique fakes weren't working. I accidentally chanced on something. Instead of throwing my fake at my partner's head, I threw my fake right next to his hand. It moved. It activated, so to speak. So I tried out a tactic. I threw a lead hand jab right beside his hand. Again it moved by reflex. It wasn't a block or parry. I did it again, but this time I followed up with a rear hand punch as a follow up. It worked like a charm. And it has worked ever since.

Right beside her hand

Example of activating my opponent's lead hand and circling over it for a back fist strike.

Attack by Trapping...

Attack by trapping is where you use some sort of obstruction or containment of your opponent's limb(s) to facilitate your attack. Any kind of grab, push, stepping on your opponent's feet will not only obstruct your opponent's counter action but again will siphon their attention units off of you and onto the trap itself. One of the things I have found about a trap is that the harder or stronger you do the trap on your opponent, the more attention units you will siphon off. I found this out when I was training with Remy Presas. He would execute his checks and trapping hands with great force. He would slam the hell out of my arms and it certainly would get my attention. I've done the same on others and it works like a charm.

For some examples I'll start off with a simple grab. The first key point to executing the grab is that it is best if your opponent has his lead hand forward enough for your to easily grab. Another is that the grab must be strong if it is to control your opponent. Lastly, the contact must be very sharp in order to grab his attention. I like to yank the arm down as I do my follow up punch.

Examples of Attack by Trapping types, a press forward (1-4) and a slap down (5-8).

The next two examples you don't see much in karate schools because of their being banned in tournaments; the leg obstruction (1-4) and stepping on the lead foot (5-8). Both, however, are excellent types of trapping.

Another kind of trapping action that I was using far in advance of the popularity of mixed martial arts is clinching up your opponent. I was a fan of boxing back in the day and I found that most karate people were not used to being tied up this way. I included several clinches in my first book, *American Freestyle Karate - A Guide To Sparring*. Methods of clinching are now far more popular these days. I like to protect myself as I come in to clinch so I'll either use a leg obstruction (shown below) or a "moving wedge" (next page) to cover myself as I enter my opponent's range.

Note that once I have secured my clinch I pull her toward me to offset her structure. From here I can knee or elbow strike her.

A "moving wedge" is aligning my knee/shin and elbow/forearm in front of me to shield me from any counter attack as I move forward. Once I have bridged the gap, I go into my clinch and attack from there.

Here is one last example of Attack by Trapping before we move on to the next category. I used this one in the school as well as in competition. Karate fighters were not used to anyone clinching back when I was competing so this was a great surprise tactic to use, especially against heavy hitters. I would close the gap and immediately grab the back of my opponent's neck and pull him forward. His reaction would invariably be to pull his head backward. I'd let him do this while keeping hold of him with one hand. When he pulled it back far enough, I would hit him in the face with the other. It worked every time.

Attack by Drawing…

Attack by Drawing is the last of the offensive approaches delineated by Bruce Lee and Joe Lewis. This is an interesting one in that you are opening up a hole in your opponent's defense by opening up a hole in yours. As opposed to Attack by Combination where you go forward to open up a hole, Attack by Drawing does the exact opposite. You entice your opponent to leave an opening for you to hit. How does this work? Simple. Any time you attack, you leave yourself open somewhere. You hit high, you leave yourself open somewhere low. You hit low and you leave yourself open somewhere higher up. We only have two arms and legs so we can't protect ourselves everywhere at once. This is the basis of Attack by Drawing.

You hit high, you leave yourself open somewhere low. You hit low and you leave yourself open somewhere higher up.

This is a higher level skill, but drilled properly, it can be played against the most experienced fighter with good effect. The key to this is to leave yourself open enough but to not be incredibly obvious about it. I am going to break that rule in the following examples just to get the point across. When you work on it, see what your partner will and will not fall for and adjust accordingly.

Note the areas we are leaving for open attack. If I leave my hands, down it opens up my head. If I raise my elbow, it opens up my rib cage. Her hands raised up in a boxer's position leaves her groin and legs open for attack.

In this first example, I drop my hands to open up my head for attack. The moment my opponent fires the punch to my head, I slide my head off to the side and counter punch the opening she leaves for me.

In this example, I leave my head open for the kick so that I can open up the groin as a target.

I used this action to win a match in Canada. I saw my opponent was set up for a front kick so how could I entice him to throw it? I dropped my hands and in came the kick. I slipped it and hit him in the face.

Attack by Drawing is based on this simple strategy: A. I want to hit the face (or any target), B. how do I get my opponent to open up that target for me? C. I'll get him to hit me low which will then open up his face. That's how I'll do it. Your Monitoring will need to be accurate so that you will see what your opponent is going to throw at you so that you can avoid being hit by it. If you are sly about leaving yourself open, your opponent will fall for this tactic without knowing that you set him up. This is the beauty about this approach.

Defensive Approaches

Hit As Your Opponent Changes...

I look at defensive approaches as responding to what your opponent does as opposed to how your are setting him up. This particular approach looks suspiciously like the Timing triggers previously outlined. Well, they are, however, you are using them as a defensive tactic this time. This particular approach can be the same as your timing for Direct Attack so how do you tell it apart? Visually you can't. The difference is in the mindset of the player. Are you an offensively minded fighter or a defensively minded one? Therein lies the difference. An offensively minded player would be thinking of this as Direct Attack. A defensive player would consider this as Hit As Your Opponent changes. In essence they are the same thing. They only differ in the mindset of the practitioner. Review the section on timing and you'll find enough examples to get you the full idea.

Hit As The Ranges Cross...

This defensive method is the next down the line in aggressiveness and was popularized by the late Bruce Lee in 1967. He even named his approach to kung fu after if, Jeet Kune Do, the way of the intercepting fist. This was quite a new approach to karate and kung fu players at the time as the standard method of defense was block and counter. It was not, however, a new approach overall as boxers had used a jab to hit someone as they approached and in fencing this tactic was called a "stop-hit".

The concept is simple. Your opponent moves toward you. You move forward and hit him as he does so. This sounds simple, yet it sounds dangerous to the person applying it. Well, it's less dangerous than it sounds and here is why. When my opponent is crossing the range to hit me, they are also timing their attack to land when they get there, not before or after.

Note that she times her attack to land by the time she reaches me. In addition, note that she has to come across the halfway point in order to hit me. This is an important point to the success of Hit As The Ranges Cross.

In using Hit As The Ranges Cross, I am stepping and striking at the halfway point between us and landing my attack before she finishes hers. This is the beauty of this approach. My attack finishes before hers does.

Now that you see that you will arrive before your opponent will, this method of defense will be easier to drill. Ensure that you are ready to move the moment you see your opponent's shoulders telegraph their initial motion. Right when you see that, you go.

I watch her shoulders to see any tell-tale movement. Her shoulders drop as she bends the knees in preparation to attack. My knees are already bent so I take off as she bends hers. I end up hitting her in mid move.

One can apply Hit As The Ranges Cross against a kick just as easily. The key is to take off before the kick is launched.

Hold Your Position and Hit...

Hold Your Position and Hit is the next down the line of aggressive forms of defense. Simply stated, you hold still and hit your opponent as he comes in. I have two distinct applications for this approach, both based on one's range. If you are taller than your opponent, you can safely use a punch as he comes in. If you are shorter, however, it is safer to use a kick as your opponent comes in at you. I'll present a demonstration of both approaches. I am taller than my partner so I can safely hold my position and counter punch.

A smaller person can use their legs effectively against a larger opponent in applying Hold Your Position and Hit. She is smaller than I am so she can safely hold her position and counter kick.

Simultaneous Block and Hit...

This is another approach that was popularized by the late Bruce Lee. The karate/taekwondo/kenpo methods of handling an attack back in the 1960s was to block it first and then counter attack. Bruce Lee introduced this concept, which he got from his base art Wing Chun Kung Fu, in 1967 in a article in Black Belt magazine. This was a revolutionary idea at the time. It has been adopted over the years an now is commonplace. What I have found to make this action more efficient is to change the emphasis around to "simultaneous hit and block". When I teach it, this makes more sense to the beginner who would continue to block first and counter attack second. The second key point I make to students is that this is an example of what I call coordinated action. In this you need to move two limbs at the same time. This requires a greater degree of coordination.

The idea here is to start your counter attack as their attack comes in at you much like Hold Your Position and Hit...

...except that you add in a block as well.

When applying Simultaneous Block and Hit, I try to keep it simple, as in the examples shown below.

Simultaneous Block and Hit is the only defensive approach where you can ignore same-siding as you aren't concerned with continuous blocking. Your counter is instantaneous.

Same side

Cross side

Block and Hit (Counter)…

I have already written quite a bit about this in the developmental stages of free-sparring. Now let's take it to its practical use. The function of a Block and Counter defensive approach is to stop the combination. It is to halt a combination attack in its tracks. There is one problem, however, and that is if your opponent has a tendency to disregard his own safety. As opposed to intelligent combinations , they throw what I call "overwhelm combinations". They steamroll right over you. I have run into opponents like this. You block and hit them and they keep coming. I found that if I really want to stop a combination, instead of Block and Counter (singular), I need to Block and *Blitz* (multiple counter blows after the block). This will stop an aggressive fighter in his tracks. So, when I think of Block and Counter, in reality I am thinking of Block and Blitz. Completely take the aggressive action away from my opponent.

Evade and Counter...

Evade and Counter is where you defend without making contact with your partner's attack and then fire a counter blow. Most people think of it as getting out of the way of an attack and yes, you do that, but I look at it differently. I look at it from a Cause and Effect viewpoint. "Getting out of the way" is an effect viewpoint. *"Holy smokes! Here it comes! Ayieeee! Phew! Missed me. Didn't get hit."* Effect. I look at from a cause viewpoint. I decide to reposition myself. *"I like it over here better. I even think I'll hit him back. Yeah, that's what I'll do."* Cause. The physical actions are the same. The mindsets are completely opposite. You will see in the examples shown that I will keep my position and alignment with my opponent as I evade. This is crucial to your success in executing this approach. Also crucial is being ready to counter fire immediately after his attack has missed you.

In this first example I slide forward at an angle causing her to miss while getting myself into range for my counter back fist strike.

196

The under kick (1-4) was a favorite of mine back when I competed. I prefer to angle step to my opponent's rear side whenever possible (5-8)

This last example is a favorite of both Keith Vitali and Mike Genova and they executed it brilliantly. They would step back prior to executing the defensive side kick. The step ensured the correct amount of distance to make this work.

Evade…

The last of the defensive approaches is simply to evade. The primary benefit to this approach is making your opponent frustrated by making him miss. It also gives you time to reset if you are caught off guard. One thing to keep in mind is whenever you evade, maintain your alignment and positioning with your opponent. Do not make him miss only to leave yourself open for his follow up attack.

Note that in the above two examples that I am aligned with my opponent, ready to block, counter or continue to evade. This is very important. What you do not want to do is illustrated below where I turn my shoulder or back to my opponent in an attempt to evade her attack. If I were to set her up for a step away side kick, then I would turn like this, but not in the course of an ordinary evasion.

By drilling the offensive and defensive approaches you will have a guideline as to what to do in free-fighting. An added benefit is that as your are familiar with the offensive and defensive approaches, you will become able to recognize which ones are your opponent's favorites. This is nearly as good as your opponent telling you in advance what his strategy is. Quite often a fighter gets into a habit pattern of successful actions. There is nothing wrong with having successful actions but when they become habits, they become very hard to switch in mid fight. This is where you can take advantage of your opponent's strengths because where they have developed strengths means there are other areas where they have not made as strong. This is nowhere near as apparent as they are in offensive and defensive approaches. Example: a very aggressive fighter usually doesn't develop his defensive capabilities to the same degree. Why? Well, his aggressiveness works well for him so why develop defense? The only problem is that against a very capable defensive fighter, that aggressiveness might not work or even work against him. Remember that earlier in the text I wrote that I was a generalist and did not specialize in any one thing? Well, my knowledge of the offensive and defensive approaches added to my abilities in the ring. I could switch from one approach that was not working to one that would work. Other fighters considered me unpredictable. That was one of the reasons why.

Here is a quote from David Levy, International Chess Grand Champion, from the April 1979 issue of Omni magazine that sums it up: *"The great world chess champion Emmanuel Lasker once said that it is not so much playing the objectively best move that is important as playing the move that is most undesirable for a particular opponent."*

That was my strategy. Do what was the most undesirable for my opponent. As you train in the offensive and defensive approaches, you will find that in the right circumstances, each one can counter the other...in the right circumstances. Against one opponent Block and Counter will work beautifully against Attack by Combination while against a different opponent Evade and Counter might just be the right move. It all depends. You will need to figure out that for yourself.

Your fighting approach, offensive and defensive, is a personal development. You will pick how you will approach free-sparring and free-fighting according to your own personality. This will, in time, gel into your own orientation point. I will describe the differences between me and one of my students. We are both champions. Each of us battle according to what fits our personalities best. It is, however, advantageous to know how any given fighter will approach a match.

Mindset...
Mindset plays a huge part in your free-fighting abilities and what kind of approach you take to it. What kind of personality are you? Are you direct and straight forward, a get it done type of person? Are you sneaky? Are you a thinker? Are you a basher? Any of these mindsets or combinations thereof will direct how you like to approach free-fighting. For example, I was a combination of a thinker and a sniper. I would observe and read how my opponent's moved, figured out what their weaknesses were and how to take advantage of them. I was not interested in getting into a slug fest with any of my opponents. Hit them and get out of there was my overall approach.

Alternately, my student, Tim Gustavson, competed in the 1990s on the national circuit. I taught him all of my strategies, all of my tricks, all of the principles I discerned from my experience in the martial arts. Tim, however, was of a different mindset. He did very well on the point karate circuit but where he excelled was in the continuous fighting division. Rather than the action being stopped when you scored on the other guy, the action continued for 2 minutes, much like a boxing match. This was where Tim's head was at. He liked to mix it up and physically dominate his opponents. He did very well at it as he won 4 National Black Belt League (NBL) world titles. The point I am making here is that each person will utilize what they learn in a different fashion according to their mindset. As karate is a martial art and not an exact science, there is no cookie-cutter approach to making every person fight the same. The principles and training methods can remain the same, but each student will apply them to their own personality and mindset.

So, the first thing to establish is what kind of mindset you have or wish to develop. Note I said "wish to develop". This is a very crucial determining factor in itself. Many people begin training martial arts because they lack self-confidence or they are afraid of what might happen if they get into a fight so they train to overcome some sort of shortcoming they have. When I was an under belt, I was deathly afraid of getting hit. My sparring method was one of hit and run. Sometimes it was just run. For a long time the only thing that was stronger was my desire to win. I remember a number of beatings I took in order to come out ahead by the end of a match. My wanting to win was stronger than my fear of getting hit. Finally, I decided to face my fear and worked through it. Now, I would still rather not get hit but I am no longer deathly afraid of it.

Types of free-sparring/free-fighting…
The earlier section titled Different Types of Free-Fighting describes for you what directions you can take in developing your free-fighting. Your mindset helps you figure out what kind of free-sparring you would like to excel in. Free-sparring is not just "sparring". Unless you are practicing no-holds barred brawling (which is useful, by the way), there are various types of free-sparring which are governed by certain rules and regulations including targets which can and cannot be hit. Since this is not a rules book I am not going to go over the minutiae of all the various rules. I'll go over them again just for clarity.

- Point fighting is where you stop and acknowledge (in some form or manner) the fact that one of the players got hit. Whoever gets in the hit or kick first scores the point.

- Continuous fighting is where the action does not stop if one of the players gets hit. They may continue hitting and defending or they may back off and look for a different opening or whatever. The key difference is there is no official stop. In America, they wear covering over the hands and feet and control their strikes.

- There is a continuous type of free-fighting in Japan (kyokushin) where it is full contact, yet has the proviso that you cannot punch to the face.

- It is the same with taekwondo free-fighting. Taekwondo fighting relies on kicking to do all the scoring and tends to stop the action if the players get within hand range. They will tend to either try to kick the other player if in hand range or push them off to get distance for kicking. Taekwondo players wear a chest protector during their sparring and completion.

- Kickboxing goes by rounds of 2-3 minutes in length and generally uses boxing gloves to protect the hands and some sort of foot padding for the feet. Targeting is generally above the waist of your opponent. You can, however, either kick the thighs of your opponent or not, depending on which association you fight for.

- Thai boxing expands on kick boxing where you use knee and elbow strikes as well as kicks to the thigh. No pads of any sort are worn except for boxing gloves.

- "Mixed martial arts" (MMA) or cage fighting is a combination of kicking, striking and grappling where you work to defeat your opponent by knock out (by way of striking or choking into unconsciousness) or submission (causing the opponent to give up the match).

Some examples of the different kinds of fighting games one can choose to participate in.

Point fighting champions Jeff Smith and John Natividad. Marcia Hall (L) first Taekwondo women world champion.

Kyokushin bare knuckle fighting.   American kick boxing champions Bill Wallace and Don Wilson.

Mixed martial arts   *Thai boxing*

These are overviews and there are variations on each of these types. As you can tell there are different types of free-sparring and each one appeals to different kinds of mindsets. So, what mindset are you or which mindset do you wish to develop? This will guide you in your training.

I was a premier point fighter who shifted over to a continuous free-fighting frame of mind after I stopped competing so I wrote this with an orientation to karate. As tactics, strategies, and principles are universal, you may find that there is a lot in this book that will apply to different types of free-fighting as well.

Okay, let's get into how you want to get the job done, the tactical approaches of how you are going to approach free-fighting. Tactics definitions include:

- The science and art of disposing and maneuvering forces in combat and

- The skill of employing available means to accomplish an end.

The definition of approach is "a way of dealing with something". When you shift from developmental sparring to free-sparring you will find by now that your partner is not going to let you walk up and hit them. This is where offensive and defensive approaches come into play.

Free-sparring, again, is training to become skilled so that one can graduate to free-fighting. Just as boxers and MMA players don't go to war every time they get into the training ring, it is the same with karate players. They spar in order to develop skills.

Free-fighting is the game of win or lose and it is a cousin to real fighting. Winning implies some sort of prize such as money, a title, a trophy, medal, or even just knowing that you won. Now here's where your tactics and strategies come into play.

Now that you are ready to free-fight, there are important factors that will play into how successful you will be in it.

- Conceptual factors: the Five Pillars (Monitoring, Timing, Positioning, Distancing, and Zanshin). These are the principles that everything I do is based upon.

- Mechanical factors: Reading Your Opponent, Footwork, Offensive & Defensive approaches, and how to effectively fake your opponent are top on the list of mechanics.

Free-fighting, however, is not just getting out there and banging or throwing everything but the kitchen sink at someone. The above factors will enable you to rise above most fighters. Without a command of them, you will be just one of the pack.

One thing I tell my students over and over is that you have to include your opponent into the equation. Your opponent is not going to stand there and let you hit them at will. They are going to try to mess you up all over the place. They are going to try to work their tactics on you. You have to include them into the equation. Okay, so how are you going to know what they are going to do? Well, you don't. But you can read their position so that you can develop a rate of prediction that will astonish most fighters.

I have a game that I play in seminars that I teach. At the very beginning, I will ask for a volunteer to come out and do some light free-sparring with me. We will bow in and right when we assume a fighting guard I will turn around and go to someone else in the room. I will tell that person what my partner is most likely to throw and what I am going to do to counter them. I go back to my volunteer to spar them. Sometimes my partner will know something is up and change his stance. If he does that I will stop again, go back to the original person and tell them what my partner has changed to do and again how I am going to counter that. I go back out and spar for a minute or so. When I am done, I ask the person I talked to what percentage was my prediction was correct. I am usually in the 97% range. How in the heck can I do that? Simple. The question is, how the heck can *you* do that?

Let's start with Reading Your Opponent. Reading your opponent can be best defined as:

- How to predict what your opponent will most likely do.

Set Point...

We are now going to take Monitoring to the next level. The concept of Set Point was taught to me by Joe Lewis. I wish I could say he took me aside and personally mentored me. It didn't happen that way. He taught this in a seminar in my home town back in 1985 and the common sense simplicity of it really hit home. First, let's take a look at the definition of "set":

- To cause to assume a specified posture or position

There are a number of sports where a player can score a goal of some sort. For my example I will use basketball. A player dribbles down the court to a position where he has an open shot to the basket. From there he throws the ball up to go through the net. Simple. Every basketball player has a certain distance and position where they to throw the ball from as well as they like to not be bothered while doing so. This distance and position is their "set point" – he's set to shoot. Of course, you have guards on the other team who are trying to not let him get to that position to shoot from.

In karate free-fighting, you have players who have certain techniques and their own way of throwing them at you. How in the heck do you know what their favorite technique is? (This will be covered in the next section called Positional Set Up, by the way.) How do you know when they are going to launch at you? Lewis had a very simple formula for this which he called Set Point.

The formula is this: Set Point is determined by two points. Your opponent is:

- Close enough to launch at you and,

- Ready to fire

Let's break them down a bit starting with close enough to launch at you. Ever since Bruce Lee talked about the importance of explosively bridging the gap (the distance between you and your opponent), fighters have been trying to develop that skill. Many fighters have figured out a distance for themselves from which they can execute this concept. They will approach that distance and then launch their attack. It's like walking to the end of a diving board. A diver doesn't dive from the middle of the board. He dives off the end. It's the same as far as where you or your opponent will launch your attack from. This is the preferred distance and it will be different for each fighter. Some will need to be closer than others. Joe used this as his measure: "Can he hit me with a kick from where he is standing? If he can, he is too close. If he is not, he will need to use some kind of footwork to get close enough." which leads us to…

Ready to fire. This one is so simple that it is often overlooked. Are his "guns" aimed at you or not? It's that simple. Take a look at this picture of Joe Lewis I've inserted. He was known for his explosive take off with his back fist strike and side kick. You will notice that both of his guns are aimed. His lead hand back fist, rear hand punch, and the edge of his lead foot (for his side kick) are all aimed at his opponent. He doesn't have his hands pointed in some other direction. His guns are aimed and ready to fire. He doesn't have to move them or reposition to get them ready to fire. They are there already.

In this first photo sequence I am not set. My hands need to be lifted up in order to fire.

The first requisite of Set Point is ready to fire. I will tell my students to look to see if their "guns are aimed". In the above photo sequence my guns are not aimed. I have to raise them to aim them and then fire. Against an experienced fighter, this will result in my action being too late. You can use this knowledge against your opponent. Are his guns aimed? Is he ready to fire without further preparation? If so, he is aimed and ready to fire.

In the above set of photos you can tell I have aimed my left fist for a punch. A good way to tell if you are aimed and ready to fire is to open your hand enough to point your index finger. If your finger points at your opponent, you are ready to fire.

The photo on the left shows my hands ready to fire yet I am too far away to launch. I have not hit my Set Point. The photo on the right shows me right at my Set Point. I am close enough to launch and ready to fire.

If your opponent is close enough to launch and ready to fire, then he is at his set point. The whole point is to not let your opponent get set or hit their set point.

How Joe described to do this was to offset them with:

- Movement or

- Fire power (attacking) before they get set

Movement is very easy. You step forward, backward, or to the side to ruin their preferred distance. When you step forward at your opponent, be prepared for his attack anyway. Your opponent might throw something at you hastily to keep you off of him. If he does so, it but it will be more of a reflexive move than a prepared attack. Stepping backward has an interesting phenomenon attached to it. I find when I step back roughly two steps, my opponent drops his guard, drops his energy, everything. It is though as if we have disconnected from him. It is a most interesting thing to observe. Fire power can be real or distractive. You go all out at them or you throw enough at them to get them off their set point. These are very simple ways to not let your opponent get set. Here are some of my notes from the seminar he gave:

What – Control your opponent's set point.
Why – Because the only time your opponent is dangerous is when they're set.
How – 1. Fire power or 2. Movement, forward or backward.
What makes up the set point?
When they get on their mark, the distance they can come forward and hit you.
When they are ready.
When you are sparring, offset your opponent before they hit their set point. Work on making your opponent miss by stepping back, stepping in, or slide stepping (to the side).

Here are some drills to aid you in developing spotting an opponent's set point:

1. Have your partner come in from out of range, set and fire. Watch where they set.

2. Have your partner come in from out of range and get into a stance. Call either "Set" or "Not set" and see if you called correctly.

3. Have your partner come in from out of range and set. You counter with movement or firepower.

4. Have your partner come in from out of range and counter before they hit their Set Point.

Let's get into Drill #1. Have your partner start out of range and come forward and set where they feel comfortable to throw an attack. They then throw the attack. You do this over and over again until you know where their Set Point is. Then you change partners and do this all over again. You do this with a number of partners.

Approach

Set

Fire

Fire

Fire

An interesting point to make is that there is the possibility of your partner having a separate Set Point for a kick and punch. It may vary by a couple of inches or so but keep on the lookout for that.

Examples of Drill #1.

You do this drill over and over and over with many different partners until you get the hang of thinking with Set Point. Once you can do this, you move on to the next drill.

Drill #2 is a very simple one. Your partner comes in from out of range and then sets. You check to see if they have hit their Set Point or not and call out "set" or "Not set". You check on two things: can they fire from their position without further preparation and are they close enough to launch. Those two criteria are what you are looking for. You do this over and over again until you have a good degree of accuracy.

Drill #3 is now where you apply the counters. Your partner starts from out of range and comes in to his Set Point. When he hits that point you either move (back, sideways - it doesn't matter) or strike at him with a kick or a punch. You are now getting used to doing something with your recognition.

Example of movement when your partner hits their Set Point in Drill #3.

Out of range

Set

Move

Somewhere along the line of reading this the thought might have come to you, *"Aren't I supposed to be moving or firing before he hits his Set point?"* Actually, yes. You are. This is where you get into Drill #4. The preceding drills are set up so that you can recognize your partner's Set Point to begin with. This is how I teach any drill. Rather than cut to the chase, I work on developing the skills in an orderly fashion. When I learned Set Point from the Joe Lewis seminar, he broke it down into these very four drills and do you know what? I was the only one who got the point! I was watching my partner and observing others in the room and they were all late. They didn't get it. What seemed very simple to me was still beyond the grasp of others. That was a very good lesson in instructing. When I teach any concept at a seminar, I will teach it "white belt style". I will teach it in the most simple of terms and drills. This doesn't come from a senior- altitude concept or anything like that. I teach drills in this fashion so that you *get* the concept. When you are in a class or seminar, you didn't go there to be confused. You went there to learn. My job is to see that you learn it, hence the simplicity of the drills involved. Okay, let's get onto Drill #4.

Drill #4 is applying denying your partner their Set Point in a controlled setting. Your partner comes in from out of range. Right before they hit their Set Point, you counter it with movement or firepower. Here is the timing key - you need to counter it just as they hit their Set Point. Remember the two key mistakes in Timing? Too soon and too late. These will be the two key mistakes in denying your partner their Set Point. If you have trouble doing this drill, go back to the preceding ones and really get them down.

I've spotted that she likes to be close before she launches. I start to move when her lead foot hits her distance. Note that her rear foot hasn't caught up so she is not ready to launch when I am moving. No Set Point.

Example of using firepower to negate her hitting her Set Point.

A good way to look at Set Point is to liken it to a sharpshooter gunning for you. You don't want him to "sight you." That's when he's got you in the cross hairs of his scope, ready to fire. When your opponent has hit his Set Point, he has sighted you. That is what you don't allow to happen, whether you move out of his sights or fire first.

Being able to spot and negate your opponent's Set Point will aid you in handling their Timing and Distancing. What about what they are going to throw? It is all nice and fine to handle their Timing and Distancing, but what they throw is going to hit and hurt you, not their Timing and Distancing. How do you handle that? The Super Dan Method has an answer for that as well.

Positional Set Up...
Remember I said in the Set Point section that I had a way of predicting what your opponent's favorite moves are? Here it is. This is what I use. "Positioning" deals with how and where you stand in relation to your opponent. Positional set up has to do with how your opponent stands in relation to you. This is another prediction tool I use. How your opponent is set up will tell you what he is most likely to throw.

When I teach this concept at seminars I make an example of its efficiency by sparring several members of the seminar, predicting what my partner will do in advance to someone who is standing off to the side. I'll square off with him, stop before any action is done, go off to the side, tell a different person (whispering) what I expect my partner to do and then go back and spar the person. I have always been 70-98% accurate. With percentages like that, you have quite an advantage. The following are what I look for.

1. Weight distribution between the feet - Most fighters have a way of tipping you off as to whether they are offensive, defensive or neutral. This is whether their weight is more on the front foot, rear foot or balanced 50-50. An offensive fighter is usually weight forward. A defensive fighter usually has their weight more towards the rear leg and a balanced fighter is usually 50-50. Weight distribution is fairly reliable, but against experienced fighters, it's the one I find the least reliable. An experienced fighter can use any weight distribution and mask his real intentions. He might rest his weight backwards to throw a lead leg kick, for example. Against less experienced fighters or fighters who are set in their ways, I find this useful. The nice thing about watching weight distribution is that a lot of fighters do not watch closely their own weight distribution so they present you with a tip of what they're going to do.

Weight forward - offensive

Weight even - neutral

Weight back - defensive

2. Aim of the front foot – This is a very good clue to what kind of front leg kick your opponent favors. I will do this drill in seminars. I will have the participants aim their lead leg straight forwards and front kick several times and then round kick from that same point position. I ask them after that which kick is easier to throw. Invariably the answer is front kick. I then have them point their front feet in a 45 degree position and have them do the same with round kick and front kick, in that order. I ask them the same question – which was easier? The answer usually ends up being round kick. I repeat the same drill having them aim the edge of their feet exactly sideways and have them compare side kick and round kick. The same question again – which is easier? Side kick is generally the answer. The sideways position can be a crap shoot as some people will throw hook kick from that exact position as well, but if your monitoring is developed, you will not be surprised by the kick.

Note the minimal amount of movement needed to execute the lead leg front kick.

Note the turning of the hips to facilitate the round kick. This is added movement and introduces extra time and motion.

The above photos show right away that the round kick from a completely forward position is comparatively inefficient. Even though the turn is slight, it introduces more time and physical motion into the kick and therefore it is telegraphed as well as slowed down in its execution. Let's take a look at the other kicks and see how the positioning of the lead foot tells us what we want to know.

Let's compare the difference in motion between a round kick and front kick when your lead foot is in a 45 degree angle point position and the round kick and side kick when your lead foot is sideways.

Kick can go off center

A key point to this is that the thigh generally turns in the same direction as the foot is pointed. This is the give away. When your thigh is pointed forward it is easiest to execute a front kick. Turn your thigh inwards a bit and you are set up for a round kick. Turn your thigh sideways to your opponent and the easiest thing to do is to kick straight at him (side kick). The foot turn creates the thigh turn which creates the telegraph of which kick your opponent wants to throw at you.

Front kick   *Round kick*   *Side kick*

Do that drill for yourself. Do not take my word for it. The purpose of this drill is for you to experience what feels the most comfortable for you to throw from which position. If you know anatomy and the natural function of body parts, this is a dead giveaway. Your foot, ankle, knee and hip are connected. When you kick, none move independently of the other. You can rotate the foot a tiny bit, but not much. As you turn the foot, you'll turn the shin, knee, thigh, and hip as well. The leg functions as a kinetic chain. If you bend your leg, pick it up and straighten it, you will see what the leg naturally does. Do the drill from the section in Monitoring and see if I'm right. If the foot is pointed forwards, the easiest kick will be front kick. If the foot is pointed inward at an angle, the easiest kick will be an angle or round kick. If the foot is pointed exactly sideways, the easiest kick for most, will be the side kick. Pigeon toe the lead foot and you'll find that side and hook kick are the usual kicks.

The pointing of the lead foot is also based on this premise: a fighter will usually never make things hard for himself to do. That is totally backwards of the aim of any endeavor. You don't learn and perfect something so that you will continue to have trouble with it. That is so simple yet it is overlooked in many areas. Why worry about what kick or punch your opponent is going to throw? He is telling you in his body position. He might as well write you a letter and mail you a check. If you learn how to read his position it is that easy. Fighters will telegraph what they want to throw by how they stand…if you know how to read them. This one is pure gold.

3. Distance between the feet - The distance between the feet of your opponent is a very good clue whether he is going to kick with his front foot or not. Here I am talking about his initial move, his kicking with the front foot without any other type of pre-kick preparation. If his feet are about one to one and a quarter shoulder width apart, count on the kick coming without footwork preparation.

If his feet are wider than that, look for a step first or the rear leg kick. If his feet are wider than one and a quarter shoulder width, he'll need some sort of step first to deliver a front leg kick. I'm talking about offensive kicking. A defensive kick can come out of a wider stance but the weight distribution will be towards the rear leg. Check it out. Put your feet in a short stance and then lead leg kick. Pretty easy. Now do it out of a deep stance without footwork set up. Good luck. See how the body goes off balance by comparison? If this happens to your body, it'll happen to another's just the same. I find that the front leg lunge kick is limited to about a shoulder and a quarter width stance. I illustrate this point on the next pages.

The further apart the feet are, the harder it is to kick with the front leg without telegraphing it.

One shoulder width apart

1 1/4 shoulder width apart

Once your feet get past 1 1/4 shoulder width apart the kick gets increasingly difficult to throw.

1 3/4 shoulder width apart

The farther apart the feet, the more likely a fighter will draw up the rear foot first before firing a kick.

So much for the front foot. What about the rear foot? How do you know if your opponent is going to kick with the rear leg? Interestingly enough, your opponent will tell you via body position. Take a look at the photos below. Note that Ashley's feet are far enough apart that her lead leg is not in the way of her kicking leg. This is a very important point. Her feet are not on a straight line with each other. In the fourth photo note the difference between her stance and mine. Mine are not set up for a front kick.

What I will look for is the pointing of the rear leg as well as if the rear leg is bent. If the knee is bent and the leg is pointed, it's most likely coming at you.

Rear knee bent

Knee & thigh aimed forward

219

A spinning kick has its own tell as well. Where a rear leg front kick will have the legs apart, a spin kick will be set up differently. The feet are lined up, more or less, one in front of the other to facilitate the spinning action of the kick.

Note how much turn she has to do from a forward facing position in order to do a spinning kick. This not only makes the kick harder to do, but it also makes it very easy to see coming.

The sideways body position makes it easy to snap your hips around for the spinning kick.

4. Hand and foot position in relationship to the Positional Center Line. This is a very slick one. Remember the earlier section on Monitoring? This is the use of how to read telegraphs by how your opponent holds his hands. If he moves his hand out away from the centerline, it's coming back at you in a hook or angle type strike. If it crosses in over the centerline, it's coming at you in a backhand fashion. If it just runs parallel to the centerline, it'll be straight at you.

How he holds his hands in regards to the centerline will tell you what he wants to throw. A lot of karate fighters hold the lead hand across the centerline. What's coming then? Backfist, of course. Take a look at your opponent's hand position. Are they up in a boxer's position? Which way do the "guns" face? From watching how your opponent sets his hands up in the first you'll see what he can throw from where he is before he even knows it. That is a nice advantage. Also, does he only have one of his hands aimed at you? One handed fighters will do that. One will be pointed and the other will be off. The pointed one is the live one.

With both Positional Set Up and watching for your opponent's Set Point, you're not only predicting exactly what they're going to throw, but also when they're ready to throw it. Positional Set Up will tell you *what*. Set Point will tell you *when*.

Footwork…

Footwork, simply defined, is the use of the legs to a) offensively get from you to your opponent and b) steps you use as your defense against an opponent's attack. I went over a couple of stepping types in the section on "Getting from point A to point B" earlier in the text. Those were the mechanics. Now let's take this to the next level and apply footwork to successful fighting.

Offensively much ado has been made about Bruce Lee and Joe Lewis extolling the need for explosive entry footwork and although I don't disagree, there are some things that must be taken into account regarding this. Explosive footwork has been promoted as the only effective footwork or, at least, the most effective footwork. This is all nice and fine except for one fact, both martial artists who promoted this idea were young men who were in prime physical shape. Bruce Lee was roughly 5' 7" and weighed 135 lbs. He was a conditioning fanatic. Joe Lewis was a larger version of Lee. He was roughly 190 lbs. and in terrific condition. For guys like them, explosive take off was not a problem. I had trouble teaching explosive take off to many of my students because they were not of the same body type as I was – lean and wiry. This led me to research footwork that would work for everybody, what I call Footwork by Range.

Footwork by range…

The offensive use of Footwork by Range is to be able to approach your opponent from any distance. Your opponent may be very good at setting and controlling the distance between him and you. Offensively the aim for you is to not get stuck into attacking from only one kind of range so that when your opponent tries this on you, so what. You'll be able to work from wherever they go. This will even mess them up more.

Defensively you can use Footwork by Range to foil your opponent's main method of entry. Usually a person will find a range they are comfortable at and then try to launch all of their attacks from that degree of closeness. When you understand exactly what types of footwork are effective from the different ranges, then you can expect the type of footwork your opponent is trying to set up for. Then you can adjust and go to a range that isn't suitable for that footwork. In other words, you mess up their attack without even touching them.

This is a list of the different types of offensive footwork you can use at the 4 different ranges of free-fighting. The objectives of learning these are to be able to recognize which range you are in at any given moment. This way you will be able to use the most appropriate method of footwork for that exact instant.

Offensive footwork…

1. Out of range - "Long" footwork: Double step, slide up-step through, multiple shuffle/slide up and so on. These steps aren't speed steps, but even-rhythm steps. Using a flow to move in from long range will enable you to change up or defend yourself when you come in, if necessary.

Grasp that concept – using a *flow* of entry.

This is the viable alternative to the explosive take off that was popularized by Bruce Lee and Joe Lewis. Depending on how much you have worked the muscles that govern sudden take offs and your body size, these two factors will determine your success using them. But not everybody can work an explosive entry. Your muscles may not be developed enough. You may be short and cannot get close enough to your opponent to make it work. There are a number of variables that might work against you. You can always apply a flowing entry. You can use these entry footwork types from the Critical Distance Line as well.

2. Critical Distance Line/Firing Line - "Medium" footwork: Slide up, spin kick, step through, spin step, switch step. At this range you can either take off at full speed or measure your entry speed to set up a forward moving defense.

3. Inside Firing Line – "Close" footwork: Lunge kick or punch, skip kick or punch. As you are inside the firing line, this is where you need to take off quickly. The one advantage to being this close is that the distance you have to cover is relatively short.

4. Leaning Touch Range - (Where you can lean forward and touch your partner): Upper body explosion.

Inside Firing Line and Leaning Touch Range you take off at full speed as you are inside the Critical Distance Line so you are in potential danger. At this range it is difficult for your opponent to react quickly enough. These are good for when you sneak into range or if your opponent inadvertently crosses into your range of hitting.

Defensive footwork...

Defensive footwork is very easy if you grasp one key idea. Your opponent is hitting at you exactly where you are at – not two feet behind you or a foot off to either side. He's aiming at you right where you are. All you need to do is to move his target slightly further away than the size of the target. You can look at this way as well. How far can your opponent reach? Let's say he can reach 3 feet from his present position. You only need to move 3 ¼ feet to make him miss then. You don't need to take large steps. His target is small. You make him "miss small". Cross reference the defensive approaches Evade & Counter and Evade.

The steps you can use are: slide back, extend back, angle step forward, side step, and spin off. You can combine any of these steps as well. A key point to make is that you do not mess up your positioning when you do the step. You want to maintain structure during transition. Keeping your structure before and after transition is easy. You are just standing there. Maintaining structure during transition means you keep your upper body the same as when you were standing still. No leaning, no waving or dropping of the arms, no turning of the body – nothing. Your legs do the moving and your upper body stays in position.

Now here is an interesting question. What are you doing when you execute a defensive step? Getting out of the way of the hit? Well, that is the result. What else are you doing? Running like a thief? Well, again, yes, but there's more to it than that which is extremely important. Let's go over something that is a bit broader in application than "running away". It is called the Connection Line.

The Connection Line...

When you square off with your opponent and are in good enough alignment to go after him, you are on what I call a Line of Attack. If your opponent is in the same position, he is on his Line of Attack. When you are squared off with your opponent and both of you are on your Lines of Attack, your lines of Attack overlap. This overlap is what I call the 'Connection Line.' You and your opponent are faced off in good alignment at each other. You are, in a sense, connected.

When you attack, your body moves across the floor in a straight line. I have never seen anyone chase anybody down by moving in a circle. Yes, you might circle around your opponent before you attack, but when you attack you go in straight at your opponent. I am talking about moving your body from point A to B, not a circular type of hit, such as a round kick or ridge hand strike. This is moving the body across the floor. You move along your Line of Attack. Your opponent moves along his Line of Attack. As I said, when your Lines of Attack are aligned or overlapped, this creates a Connection Line.

When you angle or side step as a defensive maneuver, you are getting off of the Connection Line. Your opponent will either miss his attack (if he is committed) or will need to abort and realign himself to create a Line of Attack towards you. What you are doing when you get off of the Connection Line is breaking the alignment between you and your opponent.

You are breaking and foiling his alignment with you. This puts him at effect.

This is a viewpoint shift. This is a different way of thinking. You are going back to being a cause point rather than being an effect point. When you get "out of the way of an attack" you are attempting to not be an effect. This is a type of *"Holy Smokes! Barely escaped that one! I could have gotten creamed! Whew!"* Effect is *"don't want this to happen to me"*. This is what I call fighting out the back door. A defensive step which is *"I'll decide to move over here because I'll be in a better position than he is."* is a cause viewpoint. This puts/ keeps you in a positive frame of mind, which is a very essential part of the Super Dan Method of Free-fighting.

Disconnection…

There is an interesting effect I have found that occurs when you step away from your opponent. You back off far enough and your opponent lowers his intensity and drops his guard. This is a most interesting phenomenon to observe. Obviously, the closer you are to your opponent, the more your opponent is going to be more on his guard. That is obvious. You back off and you, in essence, cut the Connection Line. You are no longer connected and your opponent feels it. He drops energy. He is not on his guard. It is interesting to observe when you spar and free-fight.

These are the two effects that you can create when you execute a defensive step. You either get off of the Connection Line to disrupt your opponent's alignment to you or you step away and break connection. Either way you maintain your advantage over your opponent.

Okay, how big does your step need to be? That all depends on what you're trying to accomplish. Are you trying to reestablish a superior position or are you trying to make him miss so that you can counter attack immediately? Those are two different goals. Obviously, if you are reestablishing a superior position or alignment with your opponent, you will want to step far enough away so that he cannot reach out and hit you.

How big does your step need to be if you are setting yourself up for an immediate counter attack? Much less than you would think. When I step to make my opponent miss, I set up for an immediate counter attack. I'll recap what I said earlier in this text. The part of your opponent's body that is going to hit you is really rather small. His fist, his foot, his elbow, are very small in proportion to his entire body. The target he is hitting at is also rather small. Your head, your belly, your groin, all cover a relatively small portion of your overall body. All you need to do is step enough to make him miss. A small step will make him "miss small". When he misses small and you retain your alignment to him, you will be in position to fire off a counter attack right away.

Broken Rhythm/Broken Flow - Deceptive offensive footwork…

Let's get back to moving in from point A to point B and insert another element into the mix. Your opponent is watching you and will see you coming at him. If you come in straight away at your opponent, he will see you. How do you handle that? Simple. You mix up your speed and energy of entry.

There is a concept that has been in the karate world since the late 1960s called "Broken Rhythm". Broken Rhythm was a term initially coined and brought to light by the late Bruce Lee. Joe Lewis later popularized it in the leading magazines of the 1970s. I had the hardest time figuring out how to teach Broken Rhythm. I learned the drills. I could do the drills. Yet I had a hard time teaching them so that others could understand them. Years later I finally found out what the problem was.

The term "Broken Rhythm" was a misnomer (def. a wrong or inaccurate name or designation). Bruce Lee's second language was English and used a term which didn't explain what he was doing. He had a misunderstood word and it was the word 'rhythm' and how it applied to fighting. So, what is rhythm in fighting? I looked it up in the dictionary.

- Rhythm – movement with a regular repetition of beat, accent, rise and fall

That didn't help at all. Nobody fights in a robotic, rhythmic beat. Fighters will fight in a continuous action or flow. A combination attack is a flow of action. Even if it an explosive flow of action, it still is a continuous action.

- Flow – a smooth, uninterrupted movement"

What I have found is that fighters have a particular rate of motion or rate of flow that suits them best. When they can dictate the fight to go at this rate, they often say they have found their rhythm or that they have dictated the rhythm of the fight.

I looked into writings about boxing. Boxers are always talking about finding their rhythm and such. Here are some examples of what I found from various sources.

"It seems having rhythm is the ability to get the opponent's timing down and being able to double up on it easily so the punches and moves can get in between the other guys punches. Or the ability to stay a quarter step ahead of his tempo."

"I think of rhythm as basically not being predictable, i.e. not throwing the same combinations, not moving your head left-right-left-right all the time. Fighting out of rhythm means a guy has more difficultly figuring you out and timing you."

"You should watch Mayweather. He is amazing at taking his opponents out of their rhythm and making them fight his fight. If you have a decent jab, use it. It is such an underused weapon in amateur boxing and it completely disrupts your opponent's rhythm if you use it right."

"Ali and Sugar Ray Leonard are beautiful to watch, I haven't seen much of Sugar Ray Robinson's fights. I see that body rhythm is putting punches together and avoiding punches make your rhythm. What in am more interested in is the defensive side of rhythm, avoiding punches and being elusive. So basically rhythm means not to be predictable with your movements and change the speed and direction of your head movements, vary the speed and combinations of your punches."

The above statements sounds like "rhythm" is basically fighting your fight and not the other guy's. The closest thing I could find as to a definition that might relate fighting was in the Oxford dictionary:

- 3.1 Art - A harmonious sequence or correlation of colours or elements

Okay, here was somewhere to begin. A *"harmonious sequence or correlation of colours or elements"* from my perspective, is fighting my fight. "Harmonious sequence" = flow. Broken Rhythm drills have always been staccato, start-stop-start affairs. Well, if fighters fight in a flow of motion then what has been called Broken Rhythm would better be referred to as Broken Flow.

Here are four basic types of Broken Flow (by no means a complete list):
- Timing break – Interruptions in a series of techniques (instead of a combination being 1-2-3-4, it is more like 1-2…pause…3-4). This can also apply to your stepping actions.
- Speed break – Speeding up or slowing down within a flow of action
- Motion break – Stopping and restarting
- Energy break – Shifting from explosive action to being relaxed or vice versa

The most common example off Broken Flow is a motion break, start-stop-restart. This is useful if your opponent likes to Hold His Position and Hit..

A fake is a Broken Flow. You start one move and get a reaction. You deliver your follow up.

If rhythm is more fighting your fight the way you want to or following your game plan, Broken Rhythm is when this is prevented. Your using a Broken Flow creates a Broken Rhythm in your opponent. Cause and effect rearing its ugly head again.

So, what is Broken Rhythm, by definition? It is when another breaks into your rhythm or interrupts your rhythm. One way is when your opponent makes you feel uncomfortable or of out of sorts by one of the four ways outlined above. You can't get the right feeling. Your rhythm is broken. Any of these could disrupt a fighter's rhythm, a fighter's composure. Then it hit me. You apply Broken Flow to *break the other guy's rhythm*. That makes sense! The term Broken Rhythm was being used backwards.

To sum it up you can break it down this way:
- Typical use of Broken Rhythm is actually Broken Flow
- Broken Rhythm as a noun is a misnomer
- As a verb it should be Break*ing* Rhythm
- Broken Rhythm is an effect, it's what the other guy feels
- As a verb it should be Broken Flow, you apply a Broken Flow to achieve a broken rhythm or upset composure

You add Broken Flow to your entry footwork and you will not need to worry about if you are explosive or not.

Two ways to use rhythm in your free-fighting...

Okay, here is a defensive application of Broken Rhythm which adheres more to the standard dictionary definition. You set up a rhythm that you can feel by bouncing up and down. The key is you need to feel the beat, the rhythm. To develop this, put on some music that has a steady beat and match that beat. Drill it until it becomes natural for you to move that way. Then you can use it defensively or offensively in your sparring. You set up your rhythm. If your partner comes at you without having matched your precise rhythm, you will feel it and you can respond. A good analogy is if you are singing a note and someone sings a different note. You can immediately hear the difference. If you get a good feel of the rhythm you set up, you will immediately feel your partner break across/into your rhythm. Note: Bouncing is not the only way to set a rhythm. It's just the easiest to describe.

I discovered this while warming up with my friend, Mike Shintaku, at a tournament. I set up a rhythm and spotted that he never matched my rhythm when he came in at me. I either hit him right away or stepped out of the way easily. I then told him what I was doing. He put it to use in his matches and won the heavyweight division. We met later in the Grand Championship match. We both use this to the extent that the crowd booed us for the apparent non-action. We were both waiting for the other to break rhythm.

Using rhythm to disguise an entry...Offensive Rhythm...

I'll use rhythm offensively as well. I'll match the rhythm my partner is setting up. I match his bouncing pattern. This creates a rapport and we are both moving as one. Without changing my rhythm I'll attack. The synchronization of your rhythms will hide your entry. You can also do this without doing a matching rhythm. You are standing there timing his bouncing. You time your take off to match his rhythm. He is doing the bouncing and your moment of entry is matched with his bouncing. If you can catch him on the up-bounce, all the better. I'll demonstrate this on the next page.

Once I have matched my partner's rhythm it is easy to move forward without her spotting until it's too late.

Note that I hit her on the up bounce.

Over To You - It's time to bake your own cake…

Let's see, what have we gone over?

- History lesson of free-fighting

- Different types of free-fighting

- Learning how to spar

- How to decipher what you perceive

- How to move

- How to attack straight away

- How to defend and counter

- How to be deceptive with your footwork

- How to be deceptive with your attacks

All right. I've given you enough ingredients to see what appeals to you and what doesn't. Now it's time for you to get to work playing mix and match.

One last piece of advice is this – take one thing at a time and work on it. Don't try to work the entire package. That will drive you nuts.

Oh, another piece of advice is if you don't understand something, get out a dictionary and look up the word you don't understand and get it defined. Remember what I said about the concept of Broken Rhythm? Well, neither Bruce Lee nor Joe Lewis took the time to look up the term to see that it didn't really apply. That caused me a ton of trouble trying to figure it out. Make life easy on yourself. If you don't understand a concept, look for a word or words you don't know the meaning of and look it/them up in a good dictionary.

Happy baking.

Prof. Dan Anderson

Appendix 1

Sparring for seniors (35 and older)...

The rest of this manual is going to be essays on various topics that will fit in with the main text but are not necessarily chapters themselves. At the tail end of this section is an interview with me. Happy reading.

I mentioned earlier in the text that I'd go over sparring for seniors. Here I go. I have had an opinion for years that *"If I could do it, anybody can."* The trick is that in order to replicate what I am doing, you need to understand what it is that I am doing. The burden of that understanding is on my head. How in the heck are you supposed to know what I am thinking unless I tell you? First, I recommend you reread this book all the way through. This book is all about sparring, and not just for seniors. How to learn to spar, how to spar safely, how to develop intelligence in your sparring – it's all there.

Second, there are a number of key points I will go over in this section that I apply to my own sparring that should make sense to you in yours.

Small stepping vs large stepping...

What is large stepping? It is the explosive lunging techniques or extended kicking techniques used in competition these days. As you get older, your muscle and tendon elasticity tends to fade. Well, mine did. There is a greater chance of injuring yourself attempting to execute these types of entries when you get older. Well, who said you had to keep doing this? Remember that Joe Lewis and Bruce Lee were young men in the best shapes of their lives when they were expounding on initial speed and explosive entry. The distance between you and your partner/opponent as not changed. Your flexibility has so change your entry with it. Using small steps may take longer for you to bridge the gap, but small steps do have an advantage. You do not rush headlong into your opponent's counter. You can observe what your partner/opponent is doing as you come forward. And if your partner/opponent moves away as you come in? No worries. You are back at square zero and didn't get hit. Patience. You will either get to him eventually or he will come to you.

These days, when I do footwork, I take small steps rather than rhythmic bouncing. I take short, random steps which keep me moving. I humorously call this the "dance of the cocoa-krispies". I do this so that I can add defensive footwork to my game. One doesn't need large steps to move a target away from an opponent. Short steps, I have found, are the key to movement and one doesn't run the risk of injuring their tendons or ankles by getting into larger motions.

Working within physical limitations...

This one is huge for senior sparring. Back in my teens through early 30s I could do it all. I could explode offensively. I could kick and punch with either side. I could double or triple kick head height with ease. I could do it all. Then, Father Time came and visited me and physical attributes began to erode. Slowly, at first and then more rapidly as the years passed. I didn't keep up with a strong training regimen after my competition days and that added the erosion. The head high kicks lowered to the midsection. The explosive offense slowed down. I gained weight. Oh boy. The tricks I could pull on everybody diminished. Super Dan was becoming "regular Dan". Well, what if you weren't Super Dan to begin with? What if you began training in karate in your 30s or 40s or older?

Earlier in this text I spoke of concentrating on what you can do and not what you can't do any more. This was a monumental mindset shift for me. For a number of years I continued to spar using experience and tricks rather than plain, simple basics. That worked for me, but when I hit my 60s, even this wouldn't work any-more. It was time to go back to basics.

Every individual body has a certain natural flexibility to it. Some people are flexible in their hips so that they can execute lateral kicks (round kick, side kick, hook kick) with relative ease. Others can't. The fascinating thing is I am talking about all ages here, not just seniors. I have seen kids whose legs were tighter than guitar strings. They have to stretch to get a kick above the waist. Okay, the point here is to take an honest inventory of what you can do with relative ease and use that as your base of operations, technique wise. Mine were front kick, straight punch, back fist and palm hook. That was it. Four moves. I based all of my footwork, strategies, and so forth on those four moves. Again, I stress that I worked with what I could do and didn't lament about what I could do no more. You'll notice that this is accent on the positive. That is key.

Defensive options need immediate counters…

This is something I found out when I worked on re-hardwiring my karate sparring. Back in the old days I had energy to spare. I used to run through a number of sparring partners in an evening's workout. One would get tired and I'd pick another. As I got older my cardio abilities lessened. I suppose that's what I get for being lazy and not keeping up a training regimen. I noticed as my cardio lessened, my sparring partner would score on me more. This presented an interesting problem. Although I am no longer afraid of getting hit, I still prefer to not get hit. I found that plain, basic defend and counter was my best option. Firing back on my partner before he could gain any momentum was the key. Instant blow back. This worked with my viewpoint of remaining at cause as much as possible when sparring. Whether I was going to block first or step to make my partner miss, my operating basis became to hit him back right away. There is nothing like a counter strike to cut into someone's offense.

Conservation of energy…

This one is a must for everyone, not just seniors. Knowing when to ramp up the speed and power is something I practiced way back in the day and is not a recent development. When I trained for tournaments I did a lot of sparring. I had a great metabolism. I would routinely run through six or seven sparring partners a night, tiring each one of them out before going on to the next one. A secret I did not tell them was that I only expended energy when I thought I could score on them. I was practicing conservation of energy before I even knew what it was! Now that I am older, I use that every time I spar. I am no the spry kid I used to be with energy to burn. Conservation of energy taught me something else – how to target my kicks and punches.

Exact targeting/technique to target…

One of the things I found in tournament competition was that people often threw techniques to non-targets. It was like "let's throw lots of stuff out there and see what lands." I was never like that. If a move wasn't meant to land, it was meant to open up a target for me. Everything had a purpose. I figured I was too small to waste techniques. If I missed I could get hit. So I developed exact targeting. A lot went into this simple concept. As I got older, it really worked for me because I didn't have that youthful energy to expend anymore.

There is a maxim an old fighting buddy, world champion Ray McCallum, uses when he spars: *"Technique to target"*. What this means is that he won't throw a technique unless he means to it hit with it. He doesn't believe in useless motions. He's either going to hit you or he isn't going to throw it. My variation that is I will throw a technique to open up a target but once I get the opening, I will commit. My key point here is that I neither have time nor energy to waste on playing around. I need to be more direct in my actions.

Short vs long techniques…

What I mean by this is that I do not go for long extensions of my kicks and punches these days. Back when I competed, everything was a bit more elongated. You could hit with an extended kick or punch and receive a point for your effort. These days I don't do that. I have two reasons. First is hitting someone with an extended technique is pretty worthless unless it is an eye jab or groin kick. Nearly all techniques need to penetrate in order to do damage. The second has to do with elasticity of the muscles and tendons (or lack thereof) when you are in your 50s or thereabouts. You will not strain or pull a muscle if you do not overextend it. That's simple. In order to not do that, your technique needs to be thrown shorter, not fully extended. Both of these points depend on you getting closer to your opponent when you fire.

Aggressive defense...

This is a concept I got from a magazine article of the first world karate championships held in Japan. Tonny Tulleners described his strategy like this: he knew that the Japanese fighters were going to be good counter punchers. He would throw his first technique knowing that it was going to be countered. His strategy was to kick and then counter the counter punch and continue firing his own punches. This strategy did him well as he won a bronze medal in the competition. My adaptation of this strategy deals with footwork. Remember my saying that not everybody has the ability to cross the gap explosively? This is the perfect alternative. Instead of trying to be faster than your opponent, you actually move forward slower. You move forward with the intention to block and counter his attack. If you have worked on your monitoring and don't go forward in a headlong rush, you will have time to see what he throws at you. If you have your arms in position, you will be able to defend as you come forward. It is a very simple concept, but it will take some practice to become skilled at. Mentally it is a bit backwards as normally, when you move forward it is to attack. Well, in a sense you are. You are just clearing the roadblocks out of the way before you hit. That's all.

Shadow boxing, mirror work, and bag work...

I practiced a lot of shadow boxing and mirror work back in my competitions days. One of my favorite boxers, Sugar Ray Robinson, said in his autobiography that the mirror shows you where your "guns" are. The mirror doesn't lie. If you think your hands are up, they might be. If you look in the mirror you will see if they are up or not. The mirror doesn't lie. It will show you if you have telegraphing or tell-tale action before you strike or not. It will show you lots of things. An interesting point I make to my students is to watch themselves in the mirror closely and to memorize how their bodies feel as they execute techniques. Once they are away from the mirror, then they should replicate the feeling. In other words, if your arms feel a certain way when you keep your hands up, replicate that feeling when not looking at yourself in the mirror. I have gotten hit way too many times by thinking that I was in a certain position when I actually wasn't. So, mirror work will tell you all sorts of things about how you are executing that your body won't tell you until you are finely attuned to it. Are your hands up or down? Are you moving smoothly or not? Do you drop your hands when you kick? The mirror will answer nearly all of your questions for you but here's the bad thing. The mirror is neither politically correct nor does it lie. Brace yourself for the cold hard truth and become a better fighter for it.

Conditioning...

If anyone is not an expert in this field, it is *me*. I had a terrific metabolism as well as a sense of when to use and conserve energy back in the day. There is one thing about conditioning that I can tell you and this is from recent experience. If you do not have the wind and energy to last you through a sparring match, you will get hit. Previously in this text I went over the concept of attention units as well as competing in a local tournament. An interesting thing happened in my first match in the 18-34 year old division. At the beginning of the match I was red hot. My focus was really there on my opponent. My Five Pillars were in. About mid-match I began to tire and something odd happened. My opponent began to catch up on the score. I didn't figure out what really happened until sometime after the tournament. As my body began to tire, I put some attention units on the fatigue and how to handle it during the match. Well, attention units on me means less attention units on him. That was just enough to turn the tide in that match. The moral of the story is the better conditioned you are, the less attention you will have on your body during sparring and the more attention you will be able to put on your opponent.

Goals…

What are your goals when you free-fight? For example are your goals to win, train cardio, have fun, develop technique, overcome fears, etc.? Knowing why you are doing it will help you attain that goal. It really doesn't matter what your goal is as it is personal to you. It is your goal so it is a valid one. Even if your goal is to go out and have fun while sparring, that's good. I've found that I get stale very quickly if I don't have a goal of some sort. I'm not a "push the body for pleasure" sort of guy. I need a reason to push the body these days. Whether it is to win a competition, work on a move, work out a theory to see if it is valid or not – whatever. I need a reason. I find most people do as well. So, what is your reason for free-sparring? Do you have one or are you running on automatic? If you are finding sparring to be a chore or you are not progressing, a goal is very key to snapping out of a slump..

Okay, a bit long-winded but I hope this helps. I've always had the view that age should not keep oneself from being able to continue free-fighting if you want to. When I tested for 9th dan, I wanted to prove that exact point. As an upper dan rank I had the option of performing in two of the four categories of the test. I opted to perform the entire test. Why? To prove to one and all that at age 60, one could roll with the younger players. Five years later I did the same thing by entering a tournament.

The key point I want to make is that age should not stop you. I hope this manual and this last section in it will aid you in continuing you on your journey.

Yours,

Prof. Dan Anderson

Appendix 2

This is an interview conducted by Ron Goin for his blog that we did in November 2012. It is one of the most thorough interviews of me in print so I am including it here in this book. DA

WARRIOR'S PATH SERIES DAN ANDERSON, MARTIAL ARTS LEGEND
by RON GOIN--RANDOM THOUGHTS

Every sport has its superstars. In the era of tournament karate, that superstar was Dan Anderson.

Dan Anderson, or "Super Dan" as he was known in those days, is a 4-time National Karate Champion, having won over 70 Grand Titles. He was featured on the cover of Karate/Kung Fu Illustrated magazine twice, and he was rated in the Top Ten lightweight fighters in the world by Professional Karate Magazine. He was rated in Karate Illustrated's yearbook Top Ten 1977, 1978, 1979 and Sport Karate 1980 in sparring competition.

He was the only competitor in America to be rated in both Black Belt magazine and Karate Illustrated magazine's Top Ten fighters of the year. 7-time national champion Steve Anderson and 3-time national champion Keith Vitali rated Dan in the Top Ten fighters of all time.

In addition to open style competition, Dan won in AAU/WUKO (Japanese organization) events including being one of the only two undefeated American Team members against the Japan National Team. He was also the first heavyweight champion in the International All-Chinese Kung Fu Championships (Vancouver, BC) fighting competition.

Dan has been recognized as being one of the most influential martial artists in the 40 year history of tournament karate. *"Dan Anderson,"* says Eric Shellenbarger, *"knows sparring inside and out."*

I never had the opportunity to see "Super Dan" Anderson fight in person, but I've met martial artists who did, and each one had a story to share. His footwork, they told me, was loose and rhythmic like a boxer. He worked angles, some said, knowing how to blitz straight in, and also how to cut in at odd angles. Forget the long, low martial arts stances seen in so many martial arts systems at the time...Dan kept his hands up like a professional boxer, and he was able to cover distances quickly. Some of the fighters from that era would move in and throw one jarring technique, but Dan threw combinations and was hard to defend against.

Dan's 1981 book, American Freestyle Karate: A Guide to Sparring, has been called *"the best I have seen on sparring,"* by none other than Loren W. Christensen.

When I ran my own school in 1982, Dan's book was required reading for my advanced students. There was so much in there, and Dan's approach seemed to blend in elements from lots of different sources...clinch work, takedowns, solid boxing and combination techniques, and plenty of good positioning work and strong kicking skills.

A Black Belt since 1970, Dan never stopped learning and never stopped expanding his martial arts knowledge. He received the prestigious joe Lewis Eternal Warrior Award in 2016. Dan has also conducted numerous seminars around the world introducing hundreds of martial artists to the Filipino Martial Arts.

I am always interested in the journey of notable martial artists, or what I consider as the Warrior's Path, and Dan graciously accepted my request for an interview.

RON GOIN: Thanks so much for taking time from your busy schedule. It's a real honor to learn more about your journey. First off, what got you started in the martial arts?

DAN ANDERSON: Two things. First of all, I was protected by my older brother, Don. He was the biggest hoodlum in the school so nobody messed with "Anderson's little brother" because nobody wanted to mess with Anderson. I had a double-0 license to be a pain in the butt…until he was sent to reform school. Once he got sent up I had to change my ways fast. So, the first reason was self-defense.

The second reason was I wanted to be cool. Bruce Lee had just come out in the TV show, The Green Hornet. This was huge. Finally, somebody who could move better than James Coburn or Steve McQueen. A real karate chopper! My mother gave in to my relentless pestering and let me do karate lessons for my 14th birthday. She thought it would be a six month fad. 46 years later I'm still enjoying my 14th birthday present. The jury is still out as to whether I am cool or not.

RG: Whatever happened to your brother?

DA: He was the perfect example of how I didn't want my life to be; drugs, crime, and finally, a prematurely ended life.

RG: What motivated you to write your book, *American Freestyle Karate*?

DA: Simply speaking, it was the book I wanted to read. There was no cohesive, comprehensive book on how to spar out there on the market. I had written one several years earlier, and I had Tuttle Publishing interested in it. But I went inexpensive on the photographs, too slow on submitting it, and they lost interest. Later on I was talking to the editor of Inside Kung Fu magazine, Paul Maslak. I'd told him that I wanted to write a book on karate sparring. I was a top-ten fighter at the time. He told me right on the spot that if I wrote it, he'd publish it. Nine months later I had the manuscript finished. I flew down to Los Angeles with my lead black belt, Bill Rooklidge, and we shot the pictures in one day. Ed Ikuta, the photographer, told me that he'd never seen anyone so organized. I had everything written down exactly how I wanted each sequence to be seen. We shot roughly 1200 photos which got edited down to about 750 or so. I have written roughly 25 books and DVDs since then. You can find these on my website www.danandersonbooksndvds.com.

RG: I used that book as one of the 'textbooks' for my own MA school in the 80's…I looked at it as one of the first mixed martial arts books on the market. Was that your intent?

DA: Not really. The MMA game was brought to the USA from Brazil in 1994. One of the things that wasn't known about me at the time is that I was a voracious student and observer of other martial arts. As a competitor I knew the rules inside and out. I always looked for an edge. One of the edges I found was that karate people were uncomfortable at the inside range. I would use knees to the groin (until they were banned) because other karate people didn't train that way. It was the same with clinching and hitting on the break. Throwing had always been a part of my training, so I included takedowns in the book. This was way before MMA, but it is interesting that it is looked upon in that way.

RG: Do you still refer to your program as American Freestyle Karate?

DA: My main curriculum for karate is American Freestyle Karate. I also teach a classical karate program (Kong Su Do) as well as Filipino martial arts--MA80 System Arnis/Eskrima.

RG: How important is style/curriculum to your program?

DA: Style/curriculum is very important as far as I'm concerned. What is considered a "style" is better stated as "system." We Americans are used to a step by step progression to skill or knowledge in anything. That is a "system". As karate is a martial "art" rather than martial "science", it is subject to personal interpretation, i.e., style. A system is dictated by the methodology by which one presents the material. Style is dictated by viewpoint. So, as an example, we could be from the same system, and yet my style might be different than yours.

RG: You were such a famous competitor during the tournament karate era. Seems like you were in every martial arts magazine I picked up during those years. How critical is competition in your view?

DA: For me, not at all anymore. The one thing good about competition is that it will put you under the stress of having to hit first. This is whether you initiate the attack or counter after the defense. Whichever way you go, you are the first to land a blow. These days that is the only thing they are good for. I've gotten very disenchanted with tournaments these days. The rules and targeting and types of techniques you can and cannot use are so restrictive that the game really restricts sparring skill. Unfortunately, many schools teach their sparring skills around what is allowed in tournaments. Back in the day, this was fine because sweeping, throwing, hitting below the belt, etc. was allowed. These days none of that is allowed.

Here is a funny example. I took my 9th degree black belt test three weeks ago. In my first free-fighting match, I hit my opponent no less than 6 times with the groin kick. This was in less than 2 minutes. I hit my third opponent in the groin as well. The only person I didn't hit was Ray McCallum, who knows how to defend against it. The two others weren't used to defending against it and this is because of present day tournament competition. You're bringing out the crabby old man in me (smile).

Here's an aside regarding my match with Ray. We fought completely different. Head butts, knees to the groin, holding and hitting, were what we did. We fought down and dirty. We used to be able to do that in a tournament back in the old days. Oh, well…

You can temper these comments with something I read one time in a book about boxing. The writer said that there's only one thing old fighters and old sports writers agree on. *"Things aren't as good these days as they used to be."* I laughed when I read that because I saw that I found myself in that category. The funny thing is that talking to fighters that preceded my generation thought the same thing so I even take my own viewpoint on competition with a grain of salt.

RG: Who would you say was your toughest opponent?

DA: That would depend on which era you are talking about. In the beginning it was Rich Mainenti. He was a kajukenbo fighter from San Leandro, California. He was the first heavyweight opponent who was crafty. He drove me nuts! In the pacific northwest, heavyweights were big guys who didn't move as fast as I did. He was as slick as they come and used head games as much as I did.

In my top twenty era it was Howard Jackson. Howard was quick. Think of him this way - his initial take off was so quick that he could get inside of Bill Wallace's chamber for his kick. I fought him twice, and he handled me easily.

In my top ten era it was Keith Vitali. Keith and I were like fighting a mirror image of ourselves. The only differences between the two of us were I was ambidextrous, but he had the greater desire to win. Each of our matches were decided by only one point.

They were all tough but those were my toughest opponents.

RG: Did you go the Professional Karate, PKA/WKA route?

DA: In the early days of the PKA I trained for full contact karate for a short while. In the Pacific Northwest there was nothing to speak of regarding fights so I gave up on that fairly quickly. I couldn't see training as hard as you had to in order to properly prepare for a full contact match just so you could possibly win $500. Not worth it. I was rated in Professional Karate magazine's top ten world lightweight fighters without having fought a single match. These were the early days and I was rated based on promise rather than actual accomplishment. Oh well.

RG: How much contact is right for competition?

DA: Strong to the body and light to the head. You've got to be able to bang to find out if you've been hit or not. Then you can figure out how to defend and know that you have to have defensive skills. You also need to know how to take a hit without you getting scattered. This is huge for self-defense training. I am big on protective hand and foot gear but I think the helmets are ridiculous. With too much padding you can get the false idea that you don't have to develop any kind of defense. Tournament karate has really gravitated towards offense and very little defense except for footwork. This is fine until you get into a corner. Then you have nowhere to run. I'm getting crabby again. Time for another question. (smile)

RG: What do you think was the impact of MMA?

DA: MMA was a severe wake up call for those of us who were stand up fighters who knew best. I wrestled for a very short time so I thought I knew how to handle a grappler and the double leg take down. The Gracies put on the first UFC and dumped ice water on our heads. They were brilliant in the marketing aspect of it. They put on a competition that is unknown in the US but has been going on for decades in Brazil. They put in the little brother who is relatively unknown to compete for the family. He's smaller than everybody else. They put fighters on the rest of the bill who have no experience (except for Ken Shamrock) in this kind of competition and then bill it as martial art vs. martial art. Absolutely brilliant! Then after several competitions they get out of the UFC before anyone can catch up to them, exiting with the PR that Brazilian Ju Jutsu is chocolate cake with both the ice cream and cherry on top. Brilliant!

That being said, it was a severe wake up call to those of us who didn't pursue the ground game at all. Here is a funny story. You'll like this. My experience with Brazilian Ju Jutsu is this. A friend of mine had a set of the Gracie tapes, and I borrowed them and began learning from them. I then experimented on my students to see if I could apply what I'd learned. The techniques worked.

Fast forward to 2004. I was teaching at Portland Community College as a substitute for an instructor who was having minor surgery. I was demonstrating a joint lock as a restraining move. I mentioned to the class that you could either restrain or break to wrist. My partner was a student who was a wrestler. He looked up at me and said, *"Or not."* I said, *"Okay, move."* He moved. He moved much faster than I anticipated and took me down. Whoops. He pinned me to the floor and said to me, *"I've got you pinned."* I looked at him and said, *"So?"* I lifted my right leg up over his shoulder and curved my back. He fell for it. He bridged and than began to try to submit me buy bending me like Gumby. Thank you very much. I wrapped my leg around the back of his neck, locked it in for a triangle choke and began to arch my back. He held the bridge and then began to tap out. Not yet. He started it. I'll decide when to finish it. About ten seconds later he dropped to one knee. I released the choke and he fell onto his back. I went over to him and said quietly, *"You made one mistake. You were out to pin me. I was out to get you."* *"You got me, coach. You got me."* This took about a minute or thereabouts. The whole class is standing there with their eyes agog. I stood up and announced that we weren't working on that today and we'll continue. That was fun.

RG: With the growing popularity of MMA, how relevant is a single-style martial arts system; i.e., karate?

DA: Utterly relevant! MMA is a sport, a rugged sport, but a sport none the less. It is not martial arts. It has moves that come from martial arts and that's all. It's a modern-day version of Roman gladiator fighting. Martial arts are governed by a martial culture. The pillars of martial culture are honor, discipline and respect. Cross training, as in MMA, is a good thing as one should be versed in how to defend yourself in all sorts of situations. Any system of karate, taekwondo, kenpo or kung fu has, besides skilled fighting ability, the development of the individual as a human being. This is the yin to the yang of fighting ability. Otherwise we are training merely fighting. I feel this (merely fighting) is the path of MMA.

RG: What do you think is in store for MMA...is it sustainable? Will it supersede boxing?

DA: MMA is going to be the new World Wrestling Federation in popularity. It definitely has the potential to supersede boxing.

RG: Is point-style karate still marketable?

DA: It was never marketable, not the point fighting aspect of it. Point-fighting is a player sport, not a spectator sport. That's why MMA has totally swamped it as a spectator sport. It is so hard to tell a winner from the loser in point-fighting. In MMA, the loser gets whupped or submitted.

Now if you're calling traditional karate or American karate "point karate", then yes, it is marketable because of the benefits beyond the physical training a student derives from the art.

RG: Let's talk about your other martial arts path...how did you get involved in Arnis?

DA: My good friend, Fred King, would bring various senior martial artists to his school for seminars. As I was a cocky point-fighter at the time, I would have no interest whatsoever. He told me about this "professor guy". No interest. He even had this "professor guy" stay with us at the California Karate Championships in 1979. I kept attempting to shine him on and blow him off but he was persistent. He finally demonstrated a self-defense technique to me, and it was then that my martial arts world changed. I'd seen all sorts of confidence in the ring. What he had was way beyond that. Right then I decided to keep my eye on this guy. About 6 months later I got to train with him. This was Prof. Remy Presas and the art was Modern Arnis. This art opened up the rest of the martial arts world for me.

RG: I noticed that you are rated as a GM in Arnis…that's very impressive…how long have you trained in FMA?

DA: I've been involved in FMA for 32 years now. I spent the first 21 years training exclusively under Remy Presas. After he passed away in 2001, I had the wonderful opportunity to train under Manong Ted Buot in Balintawak Eskrima. Manong Ted was the only student of the founder of Balintawak, Ancion Bacon, allowed to teach in his school. Manong Ted taught in the old style – one on one.

I have also had the opportunity to train with Mark V. Wiley. I haven't gotten to spend much time with Manong Ted as he lives in the Detroit area, and several years ago he had a stroke, but his influence on me is tremendous. It is the same with Mark. I've trained with him even less, but what little I have, it has changed how I do my art. From these influences I have moved from doing strictly Modern Arnis to my own curriculum, MA80 System Arnis/Eskrima.

I have taught my blend of arnis/eskrima all over the United States, the United Kingdom, Germany and the Philippines as well as authoring over 20 books and DVDs on the subject. When it comes to training these days, this is the art that I love to practice. I have a ways to go.

RG: Can one blend karate and arnis techniques?

DA: Beautifully so. What was missing from my initial training in karate was actually what was taught back in Okinawa; the joint locking, throwing, body management applications taught in the kata, weapons applications. They are all in arnis/eskrima. The first thing that Prof. Remy got across was that the arts could blend and be compatible with each other.

RG: What benefits have you derived from arnis?

DA: The first benefit from arnis training is that I went from a karate competitor to a martial artist. Arnis is far more than stick-fighting. It has empty hand actions, joint locking, throwing techniques, blade-fighting in addition to stick work.

The second benefit is that it is based on the flow rather than ballistic action. This is very important in both transitioning from one technique to the next, but also as you get older, your joints don't appreciate the hard and fast ballistic actions of modern day karate, etc.

RG: Your style of freestyle karate seems so alive and spontaneous; however, you also train in Kongsu Do… doesn't that have kata/patterns training? How important are these patterns?

DA: Kong Su is Korean-ized Shotokan karate, so yes, it does have kata. How important are the kata? Very important if you train them "correctly". Correctly is a matter of viewpoint, however. For me, if one just trains on kata without martial application, they become the same as mainstream Tai Ch'i – great exercise but don't expect to fight using what you learned.

RG: How do you free yourself from patterns? Do the patterns have combat application?

DA: First of all, kata is not free-fighting. So what we need is a little history lesson here. I'll be brief as I cover this in depth in my books on combat applications for traditional kata (*The Anatomy of Motion* and *Itosu's Legacy*).

In Okinawa, karate training is kept secret from the Japanese. In ~1903 Anko Iotsu begins teaching kata in the school system. Kara te (China hand) is exported to Japan. For whatever reason the applications are not taught or taught sparingly. Pioneers like Gogen Yamaguchi and Masatoshi Nakayama experiment with Kumite (free hands) because they are being taught "the dance" endlessly. Nakayama even said that the karate taught by Funakoshi lacked the combat feel of judo and kendo.

Kumite or free-fighting, as far as Japanese or Okinawan history are concerned, is a relatively recent development. This brand of free-fighting is exported to America. America is a boxing/wrestling nation. We are used to combat sports. Kata doesn't make that much sense. Then a wiseguy Chinese kid comes out in Black Belt magazine and says that performing kata for fighting purposes is like swimming on dry land. We know that kid as Bruce Lee. He has two things in his favor. He can move fast and he is a TV personality. America says, *"Finally! An authority who will let us fight!"* and off we go.

The golden years of free-fighting development occur and kata is thought of even less. Later in the 1990s, practitioners like George Dillman, Seiyu Oyata, Patrick McCarthy and Iain Abernethy resurrect interest in kata by showing combat applications.

What is easily forgotten is that kata was a mainstay method of training in combat karate when karate couldn't be trained in public. The key point is that when kata was opened up to the public, the applications weren't taught or were taught very watered down. Karate was for self-defense, not for sport or gentlemen's dueling.

That being said, if you restrict yourself to the set pattern (just the moves alone) of a kata, well, there is little combat value. If you don't understand how to translate the kata moves into self-defense, again there is little combat value. The trick on this is how one uses the kata in application for self-defense.

This is what I use kata for. Free-fighting is one application of karate techniques. It one training exercise, out of many, for self-defense use. Karate free-fighting, however, is dueling. It is not self-defense, per se.

Self-defense, in my opinion, is not about dueling or winning the fight. It is about getting the hell out of there. You use fighting techniques to facilitate an escape. Self-defense is not a Jackie Chan movie. You don't do battle for 10 minutes to defeat your opponent in combat. The longer you stay in a combat situation, the greater that chance for you to get injured. This is what happened to Adriano Emperado's brother. He took this guy down. The guy pulled a knife on him and stabbed him. Killed him. If I take somebody down, I'm out of here.

How do you apply the "patterns"? Simple. The usual translations of the kata actions are based on not understanding what the heck they are. Example: the rising block is taught as a defense for a punch to the head. In a kata you step forward and execute the rising block. How screwy is that for application! If someone is going to punch you in the head, they are coming to you. Why are you stepping forward to chase down the punch in order to block it? Totally backwards.

So, what is the motion involved in the "rising block"? One arm pulls down while the other one rises. Okay. If I grab my assailant's arm and move forward and ram my forearm into his neck, I've got a simple and applicable move for the "step forward rising block". My application of the kata is based on what I call Motion Application. I have written two books on this subject alone. Once you have this concept the moves of the kata become very apparent and street applicable.

RG: Does your style/academy/curriculum feature any ground fighting techniques?
DA: We have enough to get ourselves off the floor. I am of the Kelly Worden school of thought regarding ground fighting. You don't know if your assailant has a boot knife ready to shiv you when you are on the ground. Also, I am into cheating whenever I can. Example: I was at a seminar demonstrating a choke technique and got involved in a little horse-play. The guy I was demonstrating with took me down to my back. He got in a ground and pound position. I pulled him close to me for a defense. He made his mistake thinking I was going to grapple with him. I bit his stomach. He rose up and gave me enough distance to reach under him and grab him by the groin. Silly fellow wasn't wearing a cup. I picked him by the groin and tossed him to the side. He was off to the side kneeling in pain when I said to him my motto, "I cheat."

The current vogue is MMA. MMA is a sport, a very rugged sport, but a sport none the less. In MMA even the weenies are tough, but they are governed by rules, many that are inhibiting in a self-defense situation. I'll teach enough ground fighting so that a person does not freak out when they hit the floor. But it's more important to get off the floor than to finish the fight on the floor. Your attacker may have buddies who have nothing better to do than stomp you while you're dealing with his friend.

RG: I see that you tested for 9th dan last month in Texas. Isn't a rank that high usually awarded after so many years in the martial arts? Why did you test for this?
DA: First of all, in most systems a 9th dan is awarded for length of time in the art as well as contributions to the art. I had that pretty well locked, but I wanted to do something else for the art. I wanted to be a role model for those of us over 50. Martial arts are supposed to contribute to a person's longevity. I wanted to undergo a test to prove that one can do a test like that in their "advanced" years. That was the first reason. A second reason is that I have a strong senior-junior ethic. To me it is extremely improper to award yourself higher rank.

There is a colleague of mine who, when I told him that I was going to test for my 9th dan, said, *"Why test?"* Well, that might have been okay for him, but for me, no. For me to continue on up the ranks it must come from someone other than myself.

RG: You seem to have accomplished a great deal…what additional goals do you have in your MA journey?

DA: After my 9th dan test, my next personal goal is to change my own free-fighting style. I am 60 years old and "Super Dan" is someone who existed 25-35 years ago. I don't have the body to execute all the cool moves I used to do. Not a problem. My experience in the ring is such that recognizing what comes at me is not a problem. I am transitioning from a sport fighting base to a continuous, street based type of sparring. My students are adjusting to how I free-spar them.

RG: Will you pursue 10th dan?

DA: Up until my test, 10th dan was never a possibility in my eyes. My understanding of the AKBBA rules I will have to have 50 years participation in the martial arts until I would be considered for 10th dan. That's four years away. I'll think about it then.

RG: How do you stay fit? Is karate/arnis enough, or is supplemental training needed?

DA: How I stay fit is I keep active. I am not "in training" per se. In training is what I did when I competed and I am far from competition shape. I found that my preparation, cardio wise, fell short of what was needed for my 9th dan test. I got winded quite fast and then relied on experience and determination to get me through the rest of it. For me, keeping active is enough. I keep the body relatively supple through my arnis/eskrima training. If I were competing then it would be a different story. My cardio and initial move quickness would be have to be supplemented by modern training exercises such as plyometrics and so forth.

RG: As we get older some of the more athletic skills become more challenging…have you modified your program/training approach compared to your younger days?

DA: Boy, oh boy, are we ever getting older! I am relying less on athletic ability and more on the flow I got from my arnis training. For the longest time I thought I was getting lazy because I wasn't pushing the body as hard as I used to. I then read a series of interviews with senior karate players and they each spoke about how training changes as you get older. To a one they agreed that you can't train in the same manner as when you were 20 years old. Ahhhh, vindication.

Don Schollander, the first swimmer to win 4 gold medals in the Olympics has a descriptic phrase I love. He trained like a madman for the 1964 Olympics and pulled off the impossible for that time period – 4 gold medals in a single Olympics. He then went to college and didn't have the opportunity to train as hard as he had. He still competed. He called this "living off of past excesses". This means he relied on that past training for competition in the present. (If you can find his book *Deep Water*, get it. It is a terrific read.)

I have done that to the extreme. I haven't competitively trained for 20 or so years. My body has been trained, however, to the degree that I can still execute more than your usual 60 year-old martial artist. I demonstrated that last month on my 9th degree black belt test.

That being said, I do not compare myself to the current tournament fighter, body wise. They can do things these days I only dreamed of. What I can do is move within the restrictions of an older body and move with a flow rather than explosive, ballistic action. This is where the arnis training comes in. The arnis training has extended the longevity of my martial arts training beyond what many others are doing at my age. My wife is keeping me eating fairly healthily. Spiritually, my participation in Scientology is keeping me on a very even keel. All three aspects work hand in glove to keep me active in the martial arts.

[Five years later Ron submitted a number of questions to me. This was shortly prior to my promotion to 10th dan.]

RG: 10th Dan? Wow! Tell us about that process.

DA: This one was a surprise to me. I tested for 9th a number of years ago to show that one should be able to perform at some level when they reach their 60s. After I passed my 9th, I put together a thesis for 10th dan. It was a combination of several of the books I had written all detailing research I had conducted over the years. I firmly believe that there should be nothing left to faith regarding martial arts skills or performance. There should be no holes in the works, no mysteries. I hate loose ends! One of the books I wrote was my discoveries about where the street defenses skills lie in the kata. Another was how kata could positively affect your free-fighting and vice versa, how free-fighting could help your kata become better. Yet another one was how effortless martial arts could be explained and attained. I complied the print version of these along with my memoirs so that one could have a running timeline of my personal history and created a thesis out of that. Yes, I was a splendid tournament fighter but if that was all I was, I would have quit the martial arts a longtime ago. Tournament fighting was a part of my history but I've done a lot more than that and that is what I should be judged on. So, the intent of my thesis was to show the "overall Dan Anderson", so to speak.

I submitted that to Mr. Allen Steen, Mr. Roy Kurban, and Mr. Keith Yates and labelled it, *"For when you think it is appropriate."* About a month and a half ago I got ahold of Mr. Steen wanting to get his blessing for a high dan rank I was going to promote. The first words out of his mouth were, *"I read your thesis. When do you plan on moving forward?"* Well, I had submitted a cover letter to him regarding the high dan promotion I was doing so I thought he was referring to that. It took him saying that a third time to get me to realize that he was talking about me. Then I went speechless. I finally replied, *"Sir, you tell me when and where and I'll be there."* It's taken me a month and a half to get used to the idea but I'm there now.

It's fascinating in that what I had to get over was my upbringing. I began karate when I was 14 years old. The karate masters were *ancient*! They were, at least, 50 years old! LOL Well, now it has been 50 years since I began training in karate. Well, I don't feel ancient. It was a mindset that I had to get over. Whether I was worth it or not is not my call. It is the call of my seniors. Whether I am ready to accept it is my call. And as I said, it took me a month and a half to feel comfortable with it.

My view of the promotion is it is a Lifetime Achievement Award. Every year in the Academy Awards there will be a recipient of a lifetime achievement Oscar for an excellent body of work over the years. The person receiving it may not have ever won an Oscar for a single role or film they directed but the quality of their work over the years has been exemplary. This is what 10th Dan means to me. I have spent 50 years in the martial arts and I have done far more than just tournament fight, even though that is what I am primarily known for. I have trained in and achieved high rank in Filipino Modern Arnis, run a school for 32 years, have authored 50 books and DVDs on martial arts. And that is just the tip of the iceberg. 10th Dan is an acknowledgement of what I have been doing for the entire 50 years. A favorite saying of mine is *"The first five stripes are for what you take from karate. The last five stripes are for what you give back."* That says it all for me. It's the give back.

RG: Which skills/skill sets will be featured at the testing?

DA: 1. It will be a presentation, not a test. 2. I decided that I will demonstrate some of the results of my research, mostly in the area of kata and effortless self-defense.

RG: Who will be the judges?

DA: The primary judges are Allen Steen, Roy Kurban, and the American Karate Black Belt Association High Dan Board.

RG: How long did it take you to reach black belt in the first place? What was the training like when you first started out?

DA: 3 years and two months to make black. The training went from traditional kata, the usual partner line drills, and then free-sparring. The style I began in was Kongsu. This was a Korean version of Shotokan karate and predates taekwondo. The instructor of the organization trained with Taky Kimura for 6-12 months so he began to introduce some of the modified Wing Chun into the curriculum. It made for an odd fit at the time. By the time I made black belt a lot of the training was predominantly free-sparring and bag work.

RG: What is the rank progression like at your school?

DA: At my school the rough progression is White, Yellow, Orange, Blue, Purple, Green, Red, Brown and Black. It takes roughly 3-5 years.

RG: What overall skills are needed to reach black belt at your school?

DA: Strong free-sparring, street defense skills, and some kata.

RG: How about in FMA?

DA: A strong familiarization with all the basics and basic options. When I say basic options I am looking at application at different ranges. It is all too easy to work one range and then find yourself in a pickle if your partner gets too close or doesn't let you get close enough.

RG: I have visited martial arts schools which some have called black belt factories or strip-mall dojos. How do you rate the quality of the neighborhood dojo these days, and is it too easy to get a black belt?

DA: I don't comment on other schools. The odd thing is that one man's "McDojo" is another man's dream. A key point to make here is that all martial arts styles are "orientation points." How do you orient yourself in the chaos that is known as fighting? Taekwondo people orient themselves through kicking. Thai boxers have a different orientation. Master Ken restomps the groin. These are all orientation points to handle when the ca-ca hits the fan and you're in a fight. So, why is one dojo a McDojo and another is legitimate? Is the guy who is calling "school A" a McDojo from a Kyokushin background? Heck, in Kyokushin even the weenies are tough! Is the guy from the McDojo calling the hardcore training guys Cobra Kai? It ends up way too much in the way of finding ways to make someone else wrong. That sort of attitude is a complete waste of my time. My time is better spent finding more ways make my school a viable place to train to pay much attention to other schools and whether they are McDojos or not.

RG: Now that MMA and the UFC have become so prominent, is there still room for traditional martial arts schools?

DA: Absolutely! When you look at any business you will find that each business attracts a certain kind of clientele. An MMA school attracts people who want to ground and pound. Traditional or American martial arts schools attract people who want to get into martial arts for different reasons. Actually, I find it has helped me to have a BJJ school and MMA school in my area. I don't have to explain why I don't do these disciplines to people who want to train in them. They already went to the other schools.

RG: Can one still earn a decent living as a martial arts instructor?

DA: Again, absolutely! There are a couple of "ground rules" that you will need to follow. The first one is you have to service your clients. The days of *"I am the sensei and you are the maggot"* are long since gone. Back in the day when Americans didn't know any better you could run a school that way but today that won't fly.

The second thing you have to realize is that the last two to three generations are not as strong at following through when the going gets tough. They'll quit and play soccer instead...or watch Oprah or something. So, you have to be able to set your curriculum up so that you work into skill rather than demand them.

Third, in this MTV/fast food culture called the United States, you've got to keep them interested. You've got to be on your toes. Do you have ten different ways to work on the side kick? You had better or else they'll get bored and "Hey! Isn't Oprah on?"

Fourth, realize that there are very few martial artists out in the world and hardly any one of them is training at your dojo. Martial artists are a rare breed. You will have many people training in martial arts but very few martial artists. In the USA, martial arts are one activity among many. People take martial arts classes for all sorts of reasons and give lip service to being a martial artist. Sorry to be so harsh and getting up on my soapbox but there it is. There just aren't many of us around.

Making a decent living as a martial arts instructor has more to do with how to run a business and keep people interested than it does good martial arts. When you can marry the two, then you have a good dojo.

RG: What is your philosophy about sparring?
DA: Sparring is utterly essential to one's training but there are different kinds of sparring. Are you doing sport sparring? Are you street sparring? Are you sparring beginning with grabs? How are you doing this? Most sparring these days is done sport karate style. This will teach you one set of reactions and that is good. The key is why are you taking karate and then is your sparring matching that reason? If you want self-defense and your sparring is Olympic taekwondo sparing you're missing the boat.

Now, do I train in sparring? No. I have done so much sparring and research into the subject that I don't do it anymore. Well, I don't do it on a regular basis. I'll put on the gloves and knock about with the students now and again but these days I have nothing to prove.

RG: How much contact should be allowed/encouraged? Safety gear? Rules?
DA: I believe in making contact. A rule that I follow when teach is that "I don't teach my students to miss." I grew up I the no gear/no face contact days. We thought we were pulling our blows to the head but didn't realize that we were fooling ourselves once we put the gloves on. We were training ourselves to narrowly miss the target. Once we got to smack the head we had to readjust. How much contact? I think one should be able to work up to hitting the body fairly hard. You've got to make some sort of head contact no matter how light. Otherwise you can fool yourself into thinking that your defense is effective when it really isn't. There's nothing like getting hit in the head that tells you that you have to keep your hands up. Continual hard head contact I am not into. There isn't any safe way to condition the head.

RG: I recently had a discussion with a traditional martial artist...I said that kata contained "hidden" or "secret" moves. He said they're neither hidden nor secret. My argument was that since hardly anyone knows about them and must be shown, then of course they're hidden. Thoughts?
DA: How did the applications become "hidden" in the first place? I have my own theory based on human nature. The Japanese ruled Okinawa for 400 years. They had weapons and the Okinawans weren't allowed any. The Okinawans developed their own hand to hand combat systems and trained in secret. Then the Meiji era happens and Japan is interested in karate. After 400 years of being subjugated by Japan, I have a hard time believing that the Okinawans are going to openly reveal their secrets. I really do. So, a high block "protected" the head. A knife hand block "protected" the midsection and a down block "protected" against kicks. And the Japanese bought it hook, line, and sinker. Well, so did we.

The hidden moves are in plain sight but one has to know the context. In the 1960s through the 1990s there was no context for the application of kata. The high block was supposed to block head punches. The knife hand block was supposed to block midsection punches. The down block was supposed to block kicks. They didn't work but that was what they were supposed to do. Then comes along Seiyu Oyata and popularizes pressure point application of kata moves. After that George Dillman takes it to the next level of popularity. Iain Abernethy (from the UK) and Patrick McCarthy (in Japan) bring forth common sense applications of kata. I had my own realization regarding kata application which I wrote two books on the subject.

Without getting into a treatise on the subject, the hidden moves of kata are 1. Context of application (I use kata against contact, i.e. grabs and so forth) and 2. The blocks or parries are contained in the load up moves for the "blocks." What we are taught as blocks are actually strikes, catches, and joint locking actions. Check out my books *The Anatomy of Motion* or *Itosu's Legacy – The Mysteries of the Pinan & Naihanchi Kata Revealed.*

RG: Another friend of mine makes all these distinctions: Martial arts vs self defense vs sport combat vs fighting. Aren't they all one in the same, just different rules? Which one is most important?
DA: Well, they are different animals. Sport is sport and combat is combat. Yes, they have different rules but the old adage rears its ugly head, "you will fight the same way you train". So, the main thing is why are you training in martial arts to begin with? Once one is sure why one is training in martial arts, then the answer is perfectly clear. If you want self-defense, "martial arts" might not be what you want. Martial arts encompasses much more than just self-defense. Do Krav Maga instead. If you are intrigued by sport karate, ten find a sport karate school. You want to fight? Go to a school that really bangs. They aren't so much different rules but different emphasis points. The most important one is the one you are seeking.

RG: Some instructors are against students cross training with different instructors or styles. Some even prohibit attending seminars. What are your thoughts? How does one keep up to date in the latest research?
DA: I can see both points. I don't want my guys going to a taekwondo school because what I emphasize is different. I also don't want a student of mine going to a BJJ school and then having to make a choice and quitting mine. I wholeheartedly endorse going to seminars. I have learned so much from Remy Presas and Wally Jay and this was from going to seminars. People who rely mostly on YouTube, Vimeo, etc., for added martial arts info are really missing out on the hands-on experience of a live seminar.

RG: Could/can someone be 100% self-taught, what with all the books and videos and on-line training clips? What's the downside?
DA: Yes, but the training would be superficial. Who would correct you? The person doing something wrong feels he is doing it right to begin with. That kind of self-training will work only until you come up against someone who can kick your butt. Then it will fall apart like a house of cards.

RG: I know that you are a big proponent of Filipino Martial Arts. What are your thoughts on "Dog Brothers" type fighting; i.e., all out, full contact?
DA: It's like MMA. It is the most rugged game in town but it *isn't* combat. It is sport fighting complete with its set of do's and don'ts, just like MMA. Now don't get me wrong. I respect anyone who puts on the gear and goes at it wholeheartedly. In MMA and Dog Brothers type fighting, even the weenies are tough. But it is a rugged game. If you check out your FMA history, fights were measured in seconds, not rounds or minutes or hours. One sharp rap to the hand or head with a stick ended it right there. A sharp smack on the helmet to glove or meaty thigh is far different. That hurts like hell but the game can continue.

RG: Does FMA contain kata? Have you ever designed/created your own kata? What's the process like to find, learn and develop kata skills? Is bunkai important?

DA: There is no really good short answer for this. Modern Arnis does have kata but my feeling is that they were created for Americans who had kata as part of their bread and butter. The Modern Arnis empty hand anyos (kata) were NOT taught in the Philippines or Europe, only the United States. This sounds like Prof. Remy was asked again and again if Modern Arnis has any katas in it. Being very smart, Prof. Remy decided to add them to his curriculum and there you go. Other FMA systems I don't know about so I can't answer intelligently.

RG: How does one improve power with punches and kicks?

DA: In my opinion it all starts with relaxation. Once you relax you can increase the velocity of your strikes. I worked on light, snappy delivery of both kicks and punches. I am by no means a physics major but it is common knowledge that if you double the speed of your strike, you increase the impact fourfold. That's what I worked on. From there you integrate your body into any strike you deliver. Since I was a little guy I was huge on getting body rotation or momentum into my strikes. Once you coordinate your body to be in action during the entire hit, then it's time to hit the heavy bag. Joe Lewis once said something in a seminar that resonated with me. "Your body will tell you if you hit it hard or not." You can tell if you struck hard by the feeling you felt when hitting it. When you hit the bag correctly and hard, it feels relatively effortless.

RG: What about weight training/resistance training?

DA: I hated lifting weights so I didn't do it.

RG: Do you use plyometric training? If so, can you describe this training?

DA: Back in the day I never heard of it. Do I do it I these days? No. I don't have the knees for it. Would I if I were younger? Probably not. I always felt that to get skilled at sparring you needed to spar. If I wanted to get good at footwork I worked on my footwork, etc. I'm kind of a dinosaur that way.

RG: How did you stay in top condition back in the Super Dan days? Did you do roadwork? Resistance training? Can you describe your regimen?

DA: You're going to laugh at this but I did nothing really special. I hated roadwork so I didn't do it. I was blessed with a light frame and a high metabolism so I could go and go and go. One thing I was very good was how to conserve my energy. I wasted very little energy. I could go through a line of sparring partners, pooping out each one by knowing when to expend energy and when to conserve. I did lots of slow motion kicks and lots of sparring.

RG: Seems you appeared in the Nation's top fighter list all the time back, as they say, in the day. You were a true celebrity and easily recognizable with that hair, that T-shirt and that Superman logo! What was your secret to success?

DA: DESIRE! I came from a town of 24,000 people and began my karate training in a recreational center. It wasn't even a dojo! By the time I finished my first class I wanted to be the best karate guy I could be. I was voracious in my appetite for knowledge. I bought all of the martial arts magazines. I asked everybody questions. Desire. That was my personal key element to success. There is a lyric in the song Saturday In The Park by Chicago, that summed it up – *"If you want it, really want it."* That was me in a nutshell.

You've got to want it above anything else. You've got to want it beyond all the losses and upsets along the way. I didn't get married until after my tournament career was winding down. I didn't become a father until way after my tournament career was over. I didn't want my tournament career t get in the way of being the best husband or dad I could be but at the same time, I didn't want anything interfering with my tournament career, either. Was I obsessed? Yes. Was that healthy? The jury is still out. LOL

RG: Did you ever consider going in to the movies? (I'm not being factitious) or TV?

DA: That would have been fun but I didn't know any contacts in the film industry nor did I know how to make them.

RG: I remember attending a Fort Worth karate tournament back in the late 70s. It was wild. People were getting knocked down and knocked out left and right. One guy, and I'm not making this up, had a head injury where I'm pretty sure you could see the guy's skull! What was the toughest tournament in which you competed?

DA: Probably the United States Karate Championships in Dallas. I got busted up more in that tournament than any other.

RG: Did you ever get knocked out or did you ever knock someone out in a point tournament?

DA: Yes to both. I got knocked out with a spinning back fist by Rich Mainenti at the 1972 Western States Karate Championships. He had done it previously and I'd side stepped it, grabbed the back of his collar and punched the back of his head. He attempted it again. I stepped, reached out and bang! – my whole world went grey and in slow motion. I lost control of my legs and it felt like it took 20 seconds for me to hit the floor. I remember thinking about tucking my head so that I could roll backward so as to not hit my head on the floor. I watched the film of it later. I dropped like a sack of fish! LOL

Another tournament I was fighting in, around 1977 or so, I knocked out my opponent by accident. I was showboating in a match when I heard some girl shout out, *"Get him, Manuel!"* I turned away from Manuel and wagged my finger at her indicating that this was not going to happen. Thinking that I was not watching him, he took off on me. Well, I kept him in the corner of my eye the whole time. I spun and hit him in the side of his head with a hammer-fist as he charged me and he dropped like a rock. For some reason I got the point for that. I've had several incidents like that happen.

RG: Was Texas the wild West?

DA: Texas was an interesting place to compete at. It was the roughest game in town but it was also the cleanest game in town. Everybody was there to pound each other and that was the agreed upon game. There were never any hard feelings. I'll give you an example. I was in a match at Roy Kurban's tournament in Arlington, Texas 1980. I'm faking that I am going to throw a side kick. My opponent takes off at me and I hit him with a ridge hand. I wound up so much on that ridge hand that I believe it began in Oklahoma and finished somewhere in the Gulf of Mexico, intersecting his head without stopping somewhere along the way. I thoroughly rocked him. I got the point. He came across the ring, shook my hand and congratulated me on the ridge hand. The he came out like he was going to kill me. Did I piss him off? No. I just woke him up. Now he was ready to fight. THAT was Texas.

RG: I think there was a natural progression from point-style fighting to point competition with foam safety gear to full contact fighting. Lots of guys I knew made the transition. Did you see many changes to techniques as one transitioned from one type of competition to the next?

DA: Yes. The first thing that changed was people had to adjust their distance so that they were actually hitting their opponent. What was considered a controlled punch to the face was really a punch that fell short. The second thing was that many people followed the lead of Joe Lewis and adopted boxing techniques. The last thing was that most fighters stopped snapping their kicks back. Seeing that grabbing the leg and dumping your opponent was not allowed in the rules, there was no reason to retract the kick speedily so it became kick and drop. The exception, however, was Bill Wallace, but even he dropped his kicks more in full contact than he did in point competition.

RG: How did the training change?

DA: Everybody had to get in shape, learn how to honestly hit hard and how to take a punch. Roadwork and bag training had greater emphasis than before.

RG: Some guys I know ended up with lots of injuries from their martial arts days…bad knees, bad hips, etc. How did you avoid injuries? What did you do right?

DA: I remember being at a tournament in Tacoma, Washington, and seeing a classmate of mine who had knee surgery from a skiing accident. This was 1968 so the scar he had on his leg was this big Frankenstein-like scar. Very intimidating. From that point on I watched what I did. I think the key things I did to not injure myself was a) relax when I trained and b) turn my supporting foot 180 degrees away from my opponent when doing any kind of lateral kicks. I think reading a lot about internal martial arts (without training in any of them, by the way) as well as developing the flow from my Modern Arnis training has kept my body injury free.

RG: If you could go back in time what would you do differently? Any regrets?

DA: No regrets whatsoever. I've done great as well as have made some really stinker errors but I am at a point in my life where I am fine with myself. Everything that has happened to me has helped shape my current condition. If something had been different, I might not have ended up where I am now. So, no regrets, nothing I would change.

Extra Interview Questions

These are a number of questions submitted to me through Facebook. I generally allowed each person two questions.

David Battaglia: Why didn't you transition to kickboxing?

DA: In the early days of kickboxing there wasn't much money. You might make $500 on a good night but the amount of training that would have gone into making that small amount wasn't worth it. The superstars of the newly born sport, Joe Lewis, Bill Wallace, Jeff Smith and others were the marquee players. The rest of us were second string so there wasn't the incentive for me to train as hard as I would have needed to in order to compete. As it turned out it was a smart decision. I would have been in the same division as the greatest of the early kickboxers, Benny "The Jet" Urquidez. It is safe to say that he would have beaten me.

Yoon Lee: Who was your role model starting out? Who was your toughest opponent?

DA: My first role model was Joe Lewis. I remember Joe being portrayed as misunderstood and I identified with that. He was my hero until he blew me off at the 1969 International Karate Championships. Hmmm… my toughest opponent. That is a good one. There were a number of really tough opponents, each one tough in his own way.

Raymond McCallum: Who was your smartest opponent? Why? Who was your favorite opponent? Why?

DA: The smartest opponent I ever faced was a guy out of San Leandro, California named Rich Mainenti. He was Fred King's first instructor in kajukenbo. He was tricky as the day was long. My favorite opponent was Keith Vitali. Why? Because he was the number one player in the country in my Top Ten days and we were evenly matched…very evenly matched. Each of our matches were barnstormers and each were decided by only one point.

Mike George: Who is the toughest opponent you didn't fight?

DA: Two fighters come to mind, one prior to my black belt days and one during. The one prior to me becoming a black belt has to be Jim Harrison. He had to be the worst combination of a fighter one would ever face, mean and tough. During my career the fighter would have to be Jeff Smith. Jeff Was a combination of tough and very smart and I would hav loved to face him but that never happened.

Luis Fernando Jimenez: What do you consider is the most essential aspect in a fighter, mind or body. What's more important to condition in combat sport?

DA: The most essential aspect in a fighter is his mind. I have seen many talented fighters who have had terrific technique, who could do unreal things lose against less talented fighters. Why? Because they weren't confident enough or smart enough. Mental attitude is everything. As to condition, it depends if you are in a full contact/kickboxing sport or a point sport. In full contact/kickboxing conditioning is easily 70% of the physical game. You can have all the kicks and punches in the world but when you run out of gas, you run out of gas. In point fighting it is less important as point fighting is a sprint game.

Sukwinder Manhas: What are the most important attributes of a successful fighter?
Speed? Off the line explosiveness? Timing? Ability to read or create/close distance? Ability to read intent? Some or all of these or something else? ...and of course, why?

DA: Go to the Five Pillars in the early part of this book and that explains it all but here is the short answer. Ability to read your opponent's position and henceforth his possibilities and timing. Speed and off the line explosiveness are physical attributes, which of course, are important. But look at it this way. Timing can defeat speed and distancing can neutralize off the line explosiveness. They, then, are senior to those physical attributes. Now if you all of them, both the physical attributes and the overall principles, you have a very complete package.

Keith Vitali: If you were in an overtime situation, what was your go to scoring technique you could count that worked for you most of the time. I'm pretty sure it depended on your opponent, (but against someone not in the top 10 in the country) there was no guarantee move against any of them.

DA: It depends on the region. In a region where groin kicks were allowed, that was my go to move. In any other region it was my backfist strike. Either one of them worked for me the majority of the time.

John Kreng: If you're not able to see your opponent fight before you enter the ring with them, what do you do to figure them out?

DA: I would run for about the first 30 seconds of the match and let my opponent show me what his best moves were. I found out very early in the game how impatient people were. If I did nothing they would attack, usually with their best moves. That is all I would need to find out. From there I would counter them.

Darryl Santell: GM Dan I loved your story of how you met Bruce Lee. 1 If you hadn't choked on your words, what would you have liked to have asked Bruce? 2. If you were just starting in martial arts now What different style would you go into and why?

DA: You know, I have never given it a second thought. I really don't know. I think these days I'd ask him how he would transition from the explosive fighter he was in his late 20s/early 30s to a middle-aged fighter. If I were starting out in martial arts today I'm not sure. I think something softer than karate or taekwondo. I'm 65 years old at the time of this writing so I'd take that into consideration.

John Kreng: What is your thought process when you break down and analyze a fighter?

DA: The physical is covered in Positional Set Up. The mental is to see if they are a roughneck, a sniper, confident or pensive.

John Patterson: Okay, who in your whole career do you remember that you fought hit the hardest? I mean that guy that every time you saw him at a tournament you said to yourself, *"Oh no, not blaster again..."*

DA: That has to be Robert Edwards. Robert is a very good friend of mine who competed in the Pacific Northwest in the heavyweight division. He was the smoothest fighter I have ever faced. He never looked like he was hitting that hard because of how smooth he moved but that was very misleading. He hit like a mule.

Barbara Bones: How has fighting transformed your self-knowledge? In your role as the teacher, how do you talk about strategic openness. Also, how was it possible that your control of kicking contact was so precise that if my eyes were closed I would not distinguish a kick from a hand technique? How do you rob your partner of their will to win?

DA: I'll take your questions one at a time. 1. How fighting transformed my self-knowledge is that I am no longer afraid to get hit. I know that sounds a bit silly but that was a huge factor in how I trained back in the day. 2. I go over principles such as in this book more so that tactics and strategies. I no longer teach my students to compete in tournaments so that aspect has been put He was my inspiration in that respect. 4. How I attempted to rob my partner of his will to win was to play mind games with him. Quite often before a match I'd walk over to my opponent and rub the top of his head. I would talk to the crowd. Pretty much anything to make it appear that I didn't take my opponent seriously is what I'd do.

Steve Drayton: What is your favourite Professor Presas story and if you could pick only one thing, what is the most important thing you learned from the Professor? How has your FMA training influenced your Karate training and your Karate training influenced your FMA?

DA: My favorite Prof. Presas story is the one where I am doing a back and forth flow drill with him. In the middle of the drill I accidentally went into muscle memory mode and disarmed him. I thought *"Oh, boy. I really screwed up. Now he is going to kill me."* He looked at me and said, *"Danny. That was very good but your forgot one thing. I am left handed. The cane was in my right hand."* He put his cane in his left hand and we resumed the drill. He worked me over with perfect control. The lesson I learned from this was that he saw I was ready for him to up the ante. When a student pulls a fast one on me, he is showing me that he is ready to go faster, harder, more intricate. So, don't get upset. It's time to up the ante and up his training. My FMA training has made my karate much more fluid and my karate training has made my FMA much more real.

Appendix 3

My thoughts on 10th Dan...

(Note: this essay was written after my upcoming had been announced but the event had not yet occurred.) When I was first coming up, not even a black belt yet, the thought of a 10th Dan was something in the very far off and distant future. And only for the very few. As I continued on up the ranks I didn't concern myself about it because...well, just because it didn't concern me. I was doing what I thought was the correct thing to do and that was teach, research, publish my findings, try to be the best for my students, try to give back to the martial arts what I had gotten from them. 10th dan was "over there".

When I was first told of the promotion by Mr. Steen I was stunned. I was literally speechless and anybody who knows me, that is nearly impossible to do. Instead, once I get going it is hard to shut me up. I was speechless and humbled. My first thoughts were *"What did I do to deserve this? What did I do that was special?"* And I looked at what I have been doing over the last 50 years and I thought, *"Oh, that."*

A point of continued mystery for me is why I have made such a positive impact in Texas. I know I have loved competing there. I always felt it was the roughest game in town and at the same time it was the cleanest game in town. Keith Yates asked me 10 years ago when I had moved from Texas to the Pacific Northwest. I smiled and told him that I was born and raised in Washington and loved no farther than 50 miles from where I was born. I thanked him for the compliment and then asked him why he asked me that. He said that I was so well thought of in Texas that he naturally assumed that I was a Texan. My smile broadened.

My initial link to Texas came from Tacoma, Washington. His name was Steve Armstrong. Mr. Armstrong took me under his wing when I was competing as an under belt and was a mentor to me. He always felt that the Pacific Northwest had as fine of karatemen as anywhere in the country. He took me with him to my first national tournament in 1969, the International Karate Championships in Long Beach, California. This is not known by very many people but he was the one who loaned me the money to purchase a plane ticket to my fist tournament in Texas, the U.S. Karate Championships in Dallas. I surprised everyone by making it to the finals that night and made a good showing for myself. The rest, as they say, is history.

The answer to my question *"What have I done to deserve it?"* is best answered by others but one thing I am extremely proud of is my continuing research in the martial arts. I have written many books and produced many DVDs with one goal in mind – to clarify aspects of martial arts. My first book, *American Freestyle Karate: A Guide To Sparring*, was the first of its kind. It made sense of free-sparring and took it out of a mystery. My other products have had that same goal. You see, I have always had a motto, *"If I can do it, anybody can."* What I had going for me was blinding desire. I really wanted to understand the martial arts and I really wanted to become skilled. That's how I saw it.

So now 10th dan is looming in the very near future. How do I look at this? Someone earning a PhD in any area has earned that PhD. Now what he does with it is the next step. Onc doesn't earn that PhD (in physics as an example) and then shucks it to be short order cook somewhere or an electrician. One moves forward to put to use what he has learned. I will do the same.

Also, now that I will be arriving there, I see that there is a sizable strata within that number and I am an underclassman. Someone who has completed their PhD in medicine is not Louie Pasteur...yet. There is more to strive for. This is a continuance of my journey. I am honored. I am humbled. I am inspired.

My thoughts on 10th Dan part 2 (May 20, 2017)...

I've had a week since the promotion to sit back and reflect back on what 10th Dan means to me. There are many ways one can look at this rank. It can reflect the end of the line, you can't go higher. It can mean that you now have the supreme wisdom or some such. It can represent the highest skill or seniority in your particular art. It can also represent a pat on the back form the "old boy's guild". It is all in the perception and what it means to you.

I equate this rank to a life achievement award. In the Academy Awards there will be an actor or actress who will receive a Lifetime Achievement Oscar for their collective body of work and excellence over the years. Sometimes they have never won a particular Oscar in a given year but continue to turn out excellent performances year after year.

This is what 10th Dan means to me – it is an acknowledgement of what I have done and given back to the art over the last 50 years. It is a Lifetime Achievement Award, pure and simple. It is an award presented to me by the Father of Texas Karate, Allen Steen, and the High Dan Board of the American Karate Black Belt Association in recognition of a lifetime's worth of work for the betterment of karate.

I am honored by it. I am humbled by it. I am, by no means, done yet. This achievement does not mean retirement. I am 64 years old and have many years of contribution ahead of me. This award does not complete the cycle but instead spurs me on.

Prof. Dan Anderson

FURTHER STUDY
Available from www.danandersonbooksndvds

American Freestyle Karate - A Guide To Sparring

I wrote the first comprehensive book on karate sparring in 1980, which remains a classic to this day.   Reviews of readers who have bought this book include:

"Possibly The Greatest Sparring Book Available"

"Outstanding"

"This is the first book to comprehensively cover the subject of free-sparring. Written in 1979, it remains the classic text on the art of free sparring. This book is by far the finest text I have found on actually using your karate, kung fu, or tae kwon do for fighting. I felt that after reading it I actually became a better fighter; more confident, and able to read my opponents better. If there's a better book on the subject, I haven't found it sitting on a bookstore shelf yet. The material covered by Master Anderson is priceless, easy to understand and inspiring. If you are interested in taking your free-sparring to the next level, this is the book you want to get!"

American Freestyle Karate - The Master Text

Prof. Anderson wrote the first definitive text on karate fighting, *American Freestyle Karate: A Guide To Sparring*, in 1980. This book has been hailed as one of the best books on the subject of sparring. It is a staple in numerous karate school curriculums across the country.

In his newest book, The Master Text, Prof. Anderson has written the true follow up to American Freestyle Karate. Where American Freestyle Karate detailed the offensive and defensive approaches one could use in sparring, The Master Text goes much deeper into the subject. This book not only shows what to use in sparring but teaches how to spar as well.

The Master Text covers all facets of karate: sparring, free-fighting, kata, kata self-defense applications (bunkai) and combat.

Since the publication of his first book, Prof. Anderson answers what has been a question mark in the minds of karate players since the inception of karate in the United States - "What is the link between kata and free-fighting?" This question is answered in a clear cut way that applies from beginner to master.
This is, indeed, the Master Text! Reviews of readers who have bought this book include:

"The best book I found in sparring. Other books show you how to kick and punch but this book shows you also when to kick and when to punch to win in a sparring match. If you want to win in sparring, this book will help."

"I love this book. This is a great book for instructors and students alike. Dan Anderson provides a in depth program for not only learning great combinations, but also how to recognize attacks that an opponent is preparing to throw at you. Pair this with his freestyle video's and you will have years of material to benefit from."

"I bought this book for my husband for Christmas! He has not been able to put it down! He loves this book! Very informative, and easy to read!"

Fighting Tactics & Strategies: World Championship Winning Moves

After 20 years in the making, volume 2 of the best-selling book *"American Freestyle Karate: A Guide to Sparring"*, is now here. Professor Dan Anderson, a 10th Degree Black Belt, World Champion, recipient of the prestigious Joe Lewis Eternal Warrior Award and founder of American Freestyle Karate has included 20 years worth of technical viewpoints, conceptual aids and other information as well as over 50 sparring techniques. Using over 650 photos, each technique is highly detailed, including original photos taken from actual fights where these techniques were performed. This is the long awaited follow up to the longest selling book on sparring ever, American Freestyle Karate: A Guide To Sparing. This new book has been hailed as *"The master instructor's text"* on the subject.

Point! & Match! World Championship Winning Moves

Point! & Match! is the accompanying video to Fighting Tactics & Strategies and provides a visual guide to the techniques shown in the book. *"This is the first time I HAVE put on DVD all the moves that made me one of the Top Ten fighters in the US. This DVD is intended for any karate, taekwondo, kenpo or kung fu practitioner who wants to improve his or her tournament skills. Known for being a 'teacher's teacher,' I lay it all out there for you to learn.*
Disc 1 deals with the reverse punch, back fist and ridge hand. It has a special section of leg sweeps as well.
Disc 2 goes over exclusively kicking techniques for tournament competition. ALL techniques on both DVDs have been worked in competition by me personally!
This DVD set is a must for anyone who wants to improve his or her tournament skills."
Prof. Dan Anderson

Beyond Kick & Punch - The Complete Fighting Principles Of American Freestyle Karate

Beyond Kick & Punch - The Complete Fighting Principles Of American Freestyle Karate is the third book in the American Freestyle Karate series and is the culmination of nearly 40 years of research. This book strips away the complexities of free fighting and boils them down to eight fundamental principles. As principles are universal, this book is not just for the karate fighter but can be applied by any kind of fighter; from the kick/punch artist to the grappler to the mixed martial artist to the weapons practitioner. The information contained in this book can be utilized by all martial artists or all disciplines. This book contains over 800 photos in over 110 pages, this book is packed with tons of information that will be of aid to any martial artist, no matter his rank or experience.

Positional Set Up - How To Read Your Opponent Seminar (DVD)

In my competitive days, I was known as the tournament game's premier defensive fighter. Karate Illustrated magazine editor, Renardo Barden, once remarked to me, *"When you don't want to get hit, nobody can touch you."* How did I do this? By developing a method of reading my opponent which I call Positional Set Up. Positional Set Up is how to read your opponent the very moment he takes a stance. I demonstrate this at every seminar I instruct this concept at by predicting with a 97% ratio of being correct. In this DVD you will learn to read an opponent the way I do to the same result!

Notes

259

Notes

Notes

Notes

89021946R00150

Made in the USA
Columbia, SC
15 February 2018